THEOLOGY OF SPIRIT-ANOINTED WITNESS IN HOLISTIC CHRISTIAN MISSION FRAMED IN THE RELATIONAL PARADIGM

Enoch Wan &
Mathew Karimpanamannil

Cover designed by Blake Kidney

This book is part of a series on Relational Studies

Published by the Center of Diaspora and Relational Research (CDRR)
Western Seminary Press
5511 SE Hawthorne Blvd., Portland, OR 97215, USA

Printed in the United States of America

First Printing: December 2019

ISBN- 978-1-949201-04-8

✻ ✻ ✻

For more information on CDRR at Western Seminary or Enoch Wan, please visit the following sites:

- https://www.westernseminary.edu/outreach/center-diaspora-relational-research
- https://www.enochwan.com
- https://www.globalmissiology.org

RELATIONAL
Series
2

WESTERN
SEMINARY
Center for Diaspora
and Relational Research

Western Seminary Press
5511 SE Hawthorne Blvd.
Portland, OR 97215

TABLE OF CONTENTS

CHAPTER 1

INTRODUCTION

Purpose

The purpose of this book is to articulate a theology of Spirit-anointed witness in holistic Christian mission with an emphasis on relational paradigm that the church be authorized, enlightened, enriched, equipped, and empowered to proclaim, practice, and demonstrate the power of God's Kingdom. Formulating a theology of mission is not a finished task, rather an ongoing one. The place and purpose of the Holy Spirit must be emphasized in it, recognizing the Spirit's initiatory and empowering role since Pentecost for Christian witness.

Background of the Book

Co-author Mathew Karimpanamannil's theological education and pastoral ministry in India, Kuwait, and the USA enabled him to recognize the need of mobilizing the congregation of a homogenous culture for witnessing in a multi-cultural context. Teaching experience from seminaries in the past motivates him to engage in articulating a theological framework for Christian mission. Church is a comfort zone for many. In general, church members are content with church life with fellow Christians. The program-oriented church is the dream of believers. Only a small number of local congregations are actively engaged in holistic Christian mission which involves supporting overseas missions, church planting in India, street evangelism, prison ministry, assisting at the Union Rescue Mission, and routinely engaging with elderly at senior living facilities. The co-authors of this book share the conviction that a theology of Christian mission is essential in helping the church grow towards spiritual maturity and nurture church members to become responsible citizens of the Kingdom of God.

Tension emerges in churches between those who reckon mission entails active evangelism and those merely engaged in charity. The young generation is greatly influenced by ecological concerns as supreme in mission, along with recognizing equal importance of all religious traditions. Worship on Sunday has become the prime concern of members. These are content with the institutionalized nature of the church. Many become involved in mission and ministry within a secular profession. People are not motivated to have a closer relationship with God and awareness is not acquired about living the values of God's Kingdom.

Research on a theology of Spirit-anointed witness in holistic mission is a new venture that could sharpen our reflection on pastoral and teaching ministry. Jesus Christ is the perfect role model for the Church. He was aware of the anointing upon Him, proclaimed it before the people, and practiced with power (Luke 4:18-19, Acts 10:38). Scriptural foundation is needed to carry out holistic mission focusing on the Kingdom of God. It is my passion to educate the present generation to become faithful stewards of the abundant life received through the Christ-event and the Spirit-event. This research will provide the church a clear focus and right direction to be authorized, enlightened, equipped, and empowered for Spirit-anointed witness in holistic Christian mission.

Christianity and mission are inextricably interwoven throughout their history. Christian mission has developed through the centuries. Quoted in *Witness to the World*, Martin Kahler, a systematic theologian who extensively engaged in mission wrote, "Church and theology are products of mission; indeed, mission is the mother of theology." [1] Mission theology is used as a term in Christian discipline. In developing mission theology as integrative Charles Van Engen writes,

> It is helpful to speak of theology of mission rather than mission theology because fundamentally it involves reflection about God. It seeks to understand God's mission, God's intentions and purposes, God's use of human instruments in God's mission, and God's working through God's people in God's world.[2]

There are conflicting perspectives regarding mission involvement that are not easily reconciled. On the one hand, some Christians assume that all Christians are called to missions by default, as a byproduct of following Christ; on the other hand, some Christians perceive the need for a special calling similar to the Apostles in the first century. Both views are only partially true to a comprehensive understanding of the purpose and nature of Christian mission.

The Church is at peril without a sound theology of Christian mission. "We live in a world awash with mission statements, everybody is on a mission. Clearly the word 'mission' has lost its identity as a Christian term."[3] Lausanne covenant is to be asserted in this context, "We believe the Gospel is God's good news for the whole World, and we are determined by His grace to proclaim it to every person and to make disciples of every nation."[4] Commitment to the Word and the World is reflected in it. Peter Wagner writes "We evangelicals need a fresh look at supernatural power, a fresh awareness of world view, and a fresh examination of the theology of the Kingdom."[5]

We need to realize that the Christ-event and the Spirit-event resulted in a vibrant community of faith, fellowship, and witness as a sign of the Kingdom of God (Acts 2). Amos Yong writes, "Pentecost becomes the supreme symbol of the Spirit's relational power in bridging the gap between God and humanity as a whole."[6] The experience functions as an object for theological reflection. The work of

---

[1] Martin Kahler quoted in David J Bosch, *Witness to the World: The Christian Mission in Theological Perspective*, (Atlanta: John Knox Press, 1980), 138.
[2] Charles Van Engen, *Mission on the Way: Issues in Mission Theology*, (Grand Rapids: Baker Books, 1996), 23.
[3] Timothy C Tennent, Introduction to World Missions: A Trinitarian Missiology for the Twenty-first Century, (Grand Rapids: Kregel Academy Publications, 2010), 53.
[4] Ralph D Winter and Steven C Hawthorne (eds), *Perspectives on The World Christian Movement: A Reader*, 3rd ed., (Pasadena, CA: William Carey Library, 2009), 764.
[5] Peter Wagner, in Winter and Hawthorne (eds), 579.
[6] Amos Yong, Spirit-Word-Community: Theological Hermeneutics in Trinitarian Perspective, (Burlington, VT: Ashgate Publishing, 1988), 30.

the Spirit of God transcends national, ethnic, social, and other barriers and ignites Christian disciples to witness Christ.

Under the influence of materialism, modernism, post-modernism, and technological revolution, the focus of churches has drifted from Jesus Christ and mission to institutions, finances, and programs. The Laodicea syndrome (Rev. 3:14-17) plagued Christians and blinded them, which leads to spiritual and moral deterioration. The closing of Europe's churches reflects the rapid weakening of Christian faith in the West. Wide spread persecution even to the extent of martyrdom in the Middle East, African, and Asian countries is a signal for the need of consistent and courageous witness by the Spirit-anointed. The strong scriptural frame-work on theology of Spirit-anointed witness is significant in the context of various challenges Christian churches confront everywhere.

Definition of Key Terms

Key terms for the book are defined in the following list:

1. Holistic Christian Mission: an anointed act of proclaiming the Gospel of reconciliation, practicing Christian discipleship, and demonstrating the power of God's kingdom for the transformation of humanity in the spiritual, physical, psychological, and social realm in obedience to the Great Commission and Great Commandment of Jesus Christ.
2. Relational Paradigm: a conceptual model for systematic understanding that reality is primarily based on the vertical relationship between God and created order, and secondarily, horizontal relationship within the created order.[7]
3. Mission: the endeavor of both individual Christians and organized congregations to continue on and carry out the *missio-Dei* of the Triune God at both micro and macro levels, spiritually (saving souls), and socially (ushering in *shalom*), for redemption, reconciliation, and transformation.[8]
4. Spirit-anointed Witness: the dynamic act of reconciling humanity unto God in proclaiming, practicing, and demonstrating the power of God's Kingdom.

Organization of the Book

The book begins with an "introduction" (Chapter 1) followed by Chapter 2, "biblically based holistic mission in the framework of relational paradigm." Chapter 3 is "foundation and focus of spirit-anointed witness" and Chapter 4 covers the topic of "dynamic of the spirit-anointed witness: spirit-anointing." Chapter 5 deals with "message and method," with Chapter 6 covering the topic "scope and goal of spirit-anointed witness." The final chapter is a brief "conclusion."

---

[7] Enoch Wan, "A Comparative Study of Sino-American Cognitive, Theological Pattern, and Proposed Alternative," <www.enochwan.com/English/articles/relational_paradigm.html> (September 15, 2016).
[8] Wan, "Inter-Disciplinary and Integrative Missiological Research: The What, Why, and How," www.globalmissiology.org Published July 2017.

CHAPTER 2
BIBLICALLY BASED HOLISTIC MISSION IN THE FRAMEWORK OF RELATIONAL PARADIGM

Introduction

Christian missionaries need clear understanding of the value and importance of a holistic approach in ministry.

> Holistic, as a symbiotic term from the field of biology is made up of the Greek prefix *sym*, meaning inter-dependence, and a Greek morpheme *bios*, meaning "life." Here, it is best described as a relationship which is obligatory in some sense – one partner being unable to live without the other, or each depending heavily on the other.[9]

Are Christian missionaries called to minister to the entire arena of the person's need? Can everyone's problems really be met by a missionary? These questions are pertinent in a community where challenges are more, and the opportunities are less. We do receive direction from the New Testament pattern of mission. It is evident that the early Christians preached, practiced, and demonstrated based upon the convincing teachings and conduct of the Lord. In the prologue to Acts, Luke affirmed that the apostles' efforts were a continuation of all that Jesus began to do and to teach in the first volume (Acts 1:1, the Gospel of Luke).

---

[9] John Mark Terry, Ebbie Smith, and Justice Anderson (eds), *Missiology: An Introduction to the Foundations, History, and Strategies of World Missions*, (Nashville: Broadman & Holman Publishers, 1998), 517.

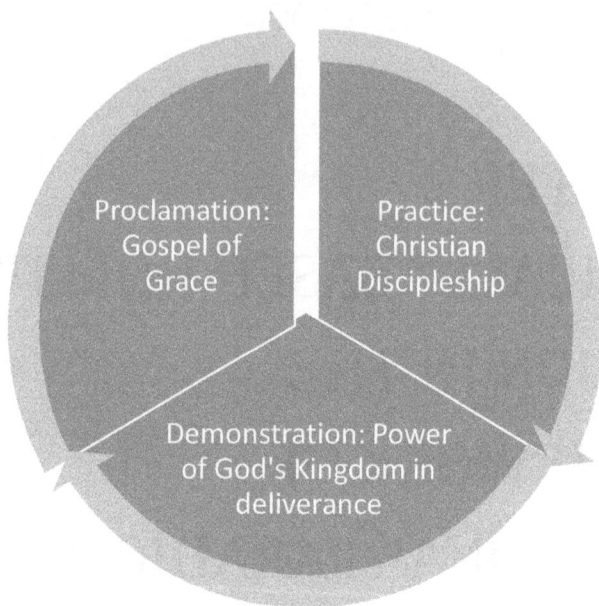

Figure 1. Biblically Based Holistic Mission

The Holistic Mission and the Relational Paradigm

The early Church continued to look back to Jesus as their model for mission. Luke records an inaugural address by Jesus at the synagogue in Nazareth (Luke 4:16-30) which is recognized as a manifesto for holistic Christian mission. Jesus declared His own sense of identity shaped by the ancient vision of Isaiah 61 in responding to God's anointing power to prophecy. He described His ministry to John the Baptist's disciples as "the blind receive sight, the lame walk, those who have leprosy are cured" (Matt. 11:4-5).

The traditional view of the authorship of Luke – Acts is that Luke, the only Gentile writer of the New Testament, wrote for Christians who are of Gentile origin. F C Overbeck, in his German commentary from 1870, confidently expressed the view as quoted by R Geoffrey Harris, "nothing could be clearer than that Acts has abandoned Jewish Christianity as such and is written from the point of view which recognizes Gentile Christianity as the absolutely dominant element in the Church."[10] S G Wilson, in *The Gentiles and the Gentile Mission in Luke – Acts*, wrote that "Luke's Church was almost certainly a predominantly Gentile Church. The influx of Jews had ceased long before, and

---

[10] F C Overbeck quoted by R Geoffrey Harris, *Mission in the Gospels*, (Eugene, OR: Wipf and Stock, 2004), 101.

the enmity between the church and Judaism had grown more bitter and the gulf wider after AD 70."[11] David Bosch, in *Transforming Mission*, supports the view that Luke was perhaps the only Gentile author of the New Testament who wrote for Christians who are predominantly of Gentile origin.[12] There are attempts to promote a Jewish Luke writing for a predominantly Jewish Church. The need for the restoration of Israel is visible in both Luke and Acts. Jesus announced His mission in the synagogue and bases it on a quotation from Isaiah (Luke 4:16-21). The Christology of Luke – Acts is Jewish and it is not framed in the form of philosophical titles, but is constructed from the Old Testament names such as King of the Jews (Luke 19:38, 23:2, 3, 37, 38, Acts 17:7), Son of David (Luke 18:38-39, 20:41), Christ (John 1:41, 4:25), Holy One (Acts 2:27), the Righteous One (3:14, 7:52), the Lord (Luke 2:11, 26, Acts 2:36, 4:26), and Servant of God (Acts 3:13, 26, 4:27, 30). Mission in the Gospels cannot be seen in isolation from the Old Testament, rather an extension from the broad mission of Israel as a light to the Gentiles. However, the Nazareth Manifesto is unique in nature and mission because of the unique anointing upon Jesus. "It was upon Him that, by an act of God, the Father, the anointing Holy Spirit was caused to rest (Luke 3:21, 22). This anointing implied that the Savior had been set apart and qualified for a task." [13] Luke's understanding of the mission of Jesus Christ as well as of the Church derives from Isaiah 61:1-2a and 58:6. The passage in Luke 4:18-19 is included here for an exegetical study to show the audience Jesus Christ's Mission.

"The Spirit of the Lord is on Me, because He has anointed Me to preach good news to the poor. He has sent Me to proclaim freedom for the prisoners and recovery of sight for the blind, to release the oppressed, to proclaim the year of the Lord's favor." "The year of the Lord" would have been understood as a reference to the year of Jubilee announced in the Torah. It is the fiftieth year, following seven cycles of seven years which have three features: (a) Debts would be canceled, (b) Slaves would be freed, and (c) Land would be returned to its original owners. Amos Yong writes, "Jesus' pronouncement that today this scripture has been fulfilled in your hearing (4:31) was therefore greeted with joy by His listeners, especially those on the underside of society."[14]

In the context of Isaiah 61 "the poor" and "the oppressed" are those in exile, who have been dispossessed, who have lost their rights and the land. They are literally in prison because they are in captivity and are subject to foreign rule and domination. In the wider context of the Old Testament and especially in the Psalms "the poor" refers to the deprived, those in need, and those who are literally afflicted or persecuted (Ps. 22:24, 34:6, 35:10, 86:1, 88:15). Isaiah is concerned to show that liberation and release are spiritual gifts as well as gifts of material freedom, and well-being. Joy and gladness are promised; song of praise instead of a spirit of sorrow (61:3). Thus, a literal release from exile is envisaged at a time when cities will be re-built, when farms, flocks, and vineyards will be given back to their rightful owners (61:4-5), and when Israel will enjoy the wealth of the nations (61:6). However, salvation is much more than material well-being: Isaiah writes, "you shall be called priests of the Lord, you shall be named ministers of our God" (61:6). Everyone will know that the liberated people are a people whom the Lord has blessed (61:9).

---

[11] S G Wilson, *The Gentiles and the Gentile Mission in Luke – Acts,* (Cambridge: Cambridge University Press, 1973), 232.
[12] David J Bosch, Transforming Mission: Paradigm Shifts in the Theology of Mission, (Maryknoll, NY: Orbis Books, 1991), 85.
[13] William Hendriksen and Simon J Kistemaker, *Luke,* New Testament Commentary, (Grand Rapids: Baker Academic, 1978), 253.
[14] Amos Yong, *Who is the Holy Spirit? A Walk with the Apostles,* (Brewster, MA: Paraclete Press, 2011), 35.

The four infinitives incorporated in it mark the nature of what Jesus was sent to do: "To preach the good news to the poor, to proclaim freedom to the prisoners, and recovery of sight to the blind, to release the oppressed, and to proclaim the year of God's favor." Traditional missions set the priority for preaching the Gospel, winning souls for Christ, and to get involved in planting churches. After Vatican II (1962-65), Roman Catholic and ecumenical protestant missions became occupied with concern for the World's poor and what ways and means could be found to liberate them from powerlessness and oppression.

Darrel Bock points out the importance of the Old Testament word *anao* as pious poor, the afflicted. God exalts those afflicted ones (Luke 1:51-53). They are the ones suffering for being open to God (6:20-23).[15] The word used in Luke 4:18 is *ptochos*. From the time of Homer in the 9th century B C, the word *ptochos* referred to the condition of being reduced to begging or asking alms. In the New Testament, it is broadened to refer to the lack of anything. David Hesselgrave has taken several texts as illustrative and insightful in this regard: (1) In the beatitudes Jesus pronounces a blessing on the *ptochoi*, referring to them as poor in spirit (Matt. 5:3). Both Matthew and Luke refer to more than circumstantial poverty. (2) When Luke speaks of the widow who put two small copper coins into the temple treasury (Luke 21:1-3), he uses the adjective *penichros* to call attention to her poverty-stricken circumstances. But when Jesus commends her in verse 3 He uses the word *ptochos*. This could indicate that what was true of her economic condition was true of her mind and heart as well. (3) When a certain woman poured costly perfume over His head (Matt. 26:6-13), some disciples complained that the perfume could have been sold and the proceeds given to the poor *(ptochoi)*. Jesus replied that the poor are always present. Obviously, poor in this instance refers to literal, circumstantial poverty. But Jesus implied in His response that His presence, death, and burial provided an opportunity greater than giving to the poor. (4) Following His ascension, Christ instructed the Apostle John to write to the seven churches of Asia (Rev. 1:17-19). To the church in Laodicea, He employed the word *ptochos* to describe the church's spiritual poverty. We may conclude, therefore, the meaning of *ptochos* is figurative and spiritual.

Sean Cordell writes in his article, "the Gospel and Social Responsibility," poor to Jesus is more than financial neediness:

In today's context it would include contributors to and results of economic poverty such as oppression by others, diseases such as AIDS, hunger, imprisonment, homelessness, those with extended joblessness, etc. (Luke 4:16-21, 6:20-26, 1 Tim. 5:10). Physical and spiritual poverty are intimately connected. Physical poverty is a fleshy depiction of the intense spiritual neediness of the human heart (Matt. 5:3-12, 1 Cor. 1:26-29, Jas. 2:5).[16]

Jesus' declaration in Nazareth incorporates four infinitives where the spiritual is primary, yet the liberation it brings is holistic. Secondly, Jesus was sent to proclaim freedom to the prisoners and recovery of sight to the blind. Prisoners are literally captives of war (Luke 21:24). Then, is this freedom physical, and socio-political? Luke nowhere presents a literal war captive being freed by Jesus. "However, a set of fragments from Cave XI at Qumran points to the likelihood that bondage to sin as well as the demonic were also part of the contemporary understanding of Captivity. Also, the

---

15 Darrel L Bock, "Luke" in *The NIV Application Commentary*, (Grand Rapids: Zondervan Publishing, 1996), 136.
16 Sean Cordell, "The Gospel and Social Responsibility" in Bruce Riley Ashford (ed), *Theology and Practice of Mission: God, the Church, and the Nations,* (Nashville, TN: B&H Publishing Group, 2011), 98-99.

word was soon used metaphorically by Christians."[17] The phrase "to the blind sight" was a recognized metaphor for receiving salvation. It is well within the compass of Luke's thinking as seen in Acts 26:18, where he describes salvation as opening eyes, and people turning from darkness to light (cf. Acts 9:8, 17-18). Also, Bartimaeus, the blind man who prayed "have mercy on me" received his sight and became a disciple of Jesus, which is an example of expectation for the church to be involved in the care of the blind (Luke 18:43).

Jesus omits the original statement of Isaiah that the Messiah would proclaim the day of vengeance. By omitting the reference to God's vengeance, however, Jesus indicates that His Jubilee year focusses on reconciliation rather than revenge, and His reconciliation is extended even to God's enemies.[18]

Instead of seeing each of the elements of Jesus messianic mission as separate we should view them as inter related aspects of His mission to restore the covenant to Israel. References include the broad spectrum of inhabitants among the lower classes of first century Palestine which constituted about 95 percent of the population, who lived under the yoke of the imperial government.

Acts 10:38-39 is a key text which highlights the theme of holistic mission with universal scope in continuation with Luke 4:18-19: Jesus Christ is the Lord of all people. It was after His baptism while Jesus was praying that God demonstrated with a dove the anointing of Jesus of Nazareth with the Holy Spirit (Luke 3:21-22).

> In contrast to Mark, Luke placed a prayer between Jesus' baptism and the descent of the Holy Spirit, thereby avoiding the notion that John's baptism mediated the Spirit and that Jesus became John's successor. The gift of the Spirit conveyed the power of healing all that were oppressed by the Devil (cf. Ps. 107:20, Isa.61:1, Luke 11:20). In His healing miracles Jesus showed Himself to be a true benefactor Who went about doing good (*Euergeteo* – Gk), the very opposite of the self-styled benefactors who abounded then as now (Luke 22:25).[19]

Both His words and actions are interpreted as actions of God through Jesus Christ in Whom God has visited His people (Luke 7:16). The peace Christ achieved is not merely for the Jews but for all people. The peace Christ wrought is the basis for tearing down the platforms of ethnic pride and the barriers of ethnic religious prejudice so that Jew and Gentile, indeed all persons, can be at peace with each other. The angel's bold declaration announced this from the very beginning of the Son's saving mission (Luke 2:10, 14). When the shattering good news that Jesus Christ is Lord of all people is heard and heeded, the church is liberated from its cultural parochialism, set free to witness across the tracks and across the World.[20]

[17] Graham Twelftree, *People of the Spirit: Exploring Luke's View of the Church,* (Grand Rapids: Baker Academic, 2009), 185.
[18] Bosch, Transforming Mission, 110-111.
[19] Gerhard A Krodel, *Acts,* Augsburg Commentary on the New Testament, (Minneapolis: Augsburg Publishing House, 1986), 197.
[20] William J Larkin Jr and Grant R Osborne, *Acts,* (Downers Grove, IL: IVP Academic, 1995), 165.

The Relational Paradigm in Great Commission

We focus on the relational nature of the Triune God as the pattern of God's mission revealed in scripture. "In the triune relationship, each of the persons of the Godhead is committed to the same purpose, and this is demonstrated in their perfect knowledge of one another, unity of will, and expression of love."[21] We also find a relational nature of mission in Jesus through the selection, equipping, and commissioning upon people who were scattered, weak, and heavy laden to provide them healing and rest. Relationship is foundational in Christian faith and practice, and a pre-requisite to systematic practical theology and missiology. Theology in a relational paradigm teaches us to look at things from a relational point of view, rather than from a legal perspective: God in three Persons in perfect union within a network of loving relationships. The incarnation of God in Jesus Christ was with the purpose of reconciling and restoring humanity from a confused and chaotic life due to the deceptive witness of Satan in the Garden of Eden. Jesus witnessed before Pilot, "I am a King, in fact, for this reason I was born, and for this I came into the world, to testify to the truth ..." (John 18:37). The Spirit-anointed witness of Jesus Christ is the supreme example for the Church to carry out the Great Commission. Enoch Wan writes, "Relational missiology is the practical outworking of relational theology in carrying out the *Missio Dei* and fulfilling the great commission."[22]

The passage referred to as the Great Commission, Matthew 28:18-20, speaks of bearing witness empowered by the Holy Spirit and making disciples of all nations. David Horner points out two trends which emerged in response to the nature of these instructions from Christ.[23] Some dilute the commission to manageable terms more suited to our preferences than to a genuine understanding of the scope of what Christ calls for us to do. It doesn't mean "while as you go, disciple the nations," rather, "go and disciple the nations." Going is not the ultimate point but a requisite, a necessary step towards the goal of making disciples. Andreas Kostenberger and Peter O'Brien address the issue in *Salvation to the Ends of the Earth*, affirming that,

> making disciples is the primary point of emphasis on the text, going is an integral part of how the exhortation is to be understood. Jesus' disciples are to go and make disciples: the aorist participle "go" (*poreuthentes*) modifies the aorist imperative "make disciples" (*matheteusate*) as an auxiliary reinforcing the action of the main verb.[24]

Others divide the Great Commission text of Acts 1:8. When efforts to highlight one to the exclusion of the others, such an inappropriate emphasis results in an imbalanced ministry. A proportional strategy targeting all those areas gives the church the opportunity to diversify its focus according to what Jesus laid out as the focus of our mission field.

Jesus' last words in the Gospel of Luke occur right after the resurrection, "He told them, 'This is what is written: The Christ will suffer and rise from the dead on the third day, and repentance and forgiveness of sins will be preached in His name to all nations, beginning at Jerusalem. You are

---

[21] Ashford, 10.

[22] Enoch Wan, "Relational Theology and Relational Missiology," *Occasional Bulletin,* vol 21, no 1, (Wheaton: Evangelical Missiological Society, 2013).

[23] David Horner, When Missions Shapes the Mission: You and Your Church Can Reach the World, (Nashville, TN: B&H Publishing, 2011), 44-49.

[24] Andreas J Kostenberger and Peter T O'Brien, *Salvation to the Ends of the Earth: A Biblical Theology of Mission,* (Downers Grove, IL: InterVarsity Press, 2011), 103-104.

witnesses of these things. I am going to send you what My Father has promised; but stay in the city until you have been clothed with power from on high'" (Luke 24:46-49). Luke's emphasis on being witnesses and the promise of power illustrate a Lukan theme: that of going to all the nations (*panta ta ethne,* all ethnicities) as witnesses in the power of the Holy Spirit. It reflects Isaiah 49:6: His people could serve as a light for the Gentiles. Paul Borthwick writes, "Luke reiterates to every ethnicity in volume one, but his emphasis is not so much on geographical expansion but rather an ethnic progression – from Jews to those separated from the Jewish community."[25] Luke describes the Gospel as repentance and forgiveness, a theme consistent with Scripture but unique in the Great Commission passages.

Acts 1:8 sets out clearly what the church is to be doing until Jesus returns: "... you will receive power when the Holy Spirit comes upon you and **you will be My witnesses** in Jerusalem, and in all Judea and Samaria, and to the ends of the earth" (**emphasis** added). Through a command-promise Jesus tells His disciples of His resources for them, that the content and scope of their primary responsibility is **"bearing witness,"** and secondarily "making disciples." The essential resource is God the Holy Spirit Who will come on them at Pentecost. Harry R Boer, who served as a missionary in Nigeria articulating well on the Great Commission regarding this passage, writes,

> "you shall be my witnesses" does not merely state what the Church would do, but what the Church would be. The great commission, as the divine mandate to the Church to be a witnessing Church, is not only a law similar to that which was set forth at the beginning of human history (be fruitful and multiply), but it is its spiritual counterpart in the new creation...The urge to witness is inborne in the Church. It is given with her very being. She cannot not-witness. She has this being because of the Spirit Who indwells.[26]

Bearing witness for God requires a person be vertically connected with God first, then witnessing horizontally to others. Life changing connection with God (being) precedes "making disciples" for God (doing). This is essentially the main feature of "relational realism paradigm" that is: vertical relationship precedes horizontal, but not without horizontal.[27] The "making of disciples" is "task-oriented" and secondary – a natural outflow of "relation-oriented" (being transformed by God).

The question by the disciples, on the restoration of the Kingdom, resulted in the declaration of the Great Commission by Jesus Christ which involves a worldwide mission. Jesus promised two things: power and witness. The future tense has an imperatival sense: "you will (must) receive power" and "you will be My witnesses" (Acts 1:8). It is an affirmation of the commission from the risen Lord at the end of the Gospel of Luke (24:47-49). The word *dunamis* is used here which is the same word used for Jesus' miracles in the Gospels. The power is supernatural and is the power of the Holy Spirit. They receive supernatural ability to work miracles and preach effectively (Acts 4:7-10, 31, 33, 6:5, 8, 8:13).[28] The endowment with the Spirit is the prelude to the equipping for mission: Spirit-anointed

[25] Paul Borthwick, Great Commission, Great Compassion: Following Jesus and Loving the World, (Downers Grove: IVP Books, 2015), 40.
[26] Harry R Boer, *Pentecost and Missions*, (Grand Rapids: Eerdmans Publishing, 1961), 122-23.
[27] Enoch Wan, "The Paradigm of 'Relational Realism,'" *Occasional Bulletin*, (Evangelical Missiological Society, Spring 2006b), 1-4.
[28] Larkin Jr and Osborne, 41.

witness (*martys*). In Acts, witness is to the earthly ministry of Jesus and to His resurrection (1:22, 2:32, 3:15, 5:32, 10:39-41).

Acts 1:8 provides the outline of the book of Acts which includes the horizontal aspect in relational paradigm with the geographical scope in mission: Jerusalem (1-7), Judea and Samaria (8-12), the ends of the earth (13-28).

John B Polhill writes regarding the witness,

> it is not by accident that Jerusalem came first. Jerusalem was central, from the temple scenes of the infancy narrative, to the long central journey to Jerusalem (Luke 9:51-19:28), to Jesus' passion in the city that killed its prophets (13:34). The story of Jesus led to Jerusalem; the story of the church led from Jerusalem. Judea was understood in the sense of the Davidic Kingdom, which would include the coastal territories and Galilee as well. Samaria is mentioned separately because of its non-Jewish constituency. Rome is not the end of the earth but the center of the empire from which all roads lead to the end of the earth. Paul's proclamation in Rome guaranteed that the normative witness enshrined in Luke-Acts will reach the end of the earth. Therefore, Acts concludes in an open-ended way, and the final mandate of Jesus of 1:8 calls the church to continue the task of carrying the apostolic witness to the end of the earth, even as Paul carried it to Asia minor, Greece, and Rome. The phrase is often found in the prophets, however, as an expression for distant lands; and such is the meaning in Isaiah 49:6. Paul's preaching without hindrance in Rome (Acts.28:31) suggests that the story has not reached its final destination – the witness continues.[29]

There is a traditional interpretation that the disciples were instantly sent out to fulfill the Great Commission. This may not be correct by analyzing the account in Acts of the Apostles. "The alternate thesis is that a whole series of events, pushed by the Holy Spirit, led in a certain direction."[30] Though the missionary story begins with Pentecost and its impact is universality, the church after Pentecost was still a faithful sect completely within Judaism. They met daily in the temple and included many priests in their membership (Acts 6:7). Here is the Palestinian messianic sect that believed they knew who the Messiah was, that He had come, that after being killed He was raised, and that He was the center of their gathering. These were committed to fulfilling the entire law as interpreted by their rabbinic tradition. They included in their number priests and Pharisees (Acts 6:7, 15:5). These sent people two by two, to other churches that they had not founded, to observe how the law was being kept. The second party was the Hellenists. They were equally as Jewish as the Palestinians, yet with wider cultural horizons. The Hellenists had been living in other parts of the World, sometimes for generations. These would come back to Jerusalem for religious feasts when they could. They were living in Corinth, Ephesus, Tarsus, and elsewhere. These Hellenists lived their life of faith normally in the synagogues located where they resided. The synagogue focused on scripture not on the ritual or sacrifice. The synagogue's cultural form was congregational and local, not central and hierarchical. Stephen did his preaching in the Hellenistic synagogues (Acts 6-7). Hellenistic Jews were more Jewish because their Jewishness had been tested and confirmed in the wider World, choosing to stay Jewish in a pagan culture. We find the sociological context for the tensions regarding the Hellenistic widows

---

[29] John B Polhill, *Acts*, The New American Commentary 26 (Nashville, TN: Broadman Press, 1992), 86.
[30] John Howard Yoder, *Theology of Mission*, (Downers Grove: IVP Academic, 2014), 80.

in Chapter 6. They were Greek-speaking Jews who had lived outside of Palestine and came back to Jerusalem to retire. They were not well taken care of like Palestinian Jewish widows though the gathering of followers of Jesus in Acts also included widows for special care. Hellenistic Jewish Christians were the first people to spread the Gospel beyond Jerusalem. The story of this movement begins with Stephen's discourse in Acts 7. This speech represents the new perspective that the Hellenistic Jewish Christians brought into the Church. The discourse begins by critiquing temple-oriented worship. The first wave of persecution arose against the church (Acts 8:1-3). The second person who carried this outward movement was Philip. He was one of those scattered in the Hellenist persecution and he turned up in Samaria. Philip shared the faith with them. The Holy Spirit worked again to confirm the Gospel. "Peter and John came from Jerusalem to see whether Samaritans coming to faith in Christ was all right, and they concluded affirmatively because again there were signs and wonders."[31]

The story's next step is again a story of broadening (Acts 10-11). The whole story is about Peter's resistance and change. "The Cornelius event" is a major turning point in the book. Peter was open to a wider mission than the Pharisees in the Church (Acts 15:5). After Cornelius' story, we find the scattered Hellenists in Antioch. They were the first to preach to pagan Gentiles (Acts 11:19-21), i.e. inter-cultural and inter-racial evangelism. In Antioch, they were first called "Christians" (11:25-27). It was to be the base for Paul's mission. Paul's pivotal role in the story of the Jerusalem Council in Chapter 15 also resulted in providing right direction for the Church to grow geographically and cross-culturally for the expansion of Christianity. In the story of Acts, however, the Holy Spirit pushes people and the Church beyond the present boarders of their community and broadened their horizon. The Holy Spirit makes mission happen, and makes mission acceptable,

> The reason the Church in Jerusalem had to accept Peter's report about Cornelius was that they too had had ecstatic experience: accredited a new breakthrough. The Spirit does not just empower the preacher to prepare the listener and bring the listener to assurance. The Spirit does both of those and in addition gives orders to the community.[32]

Hence, we witnessed the **vertical interaction** of the Holy Spirit empowering and guiding the early church to **expand horizontally** beyond geographic, cultural, and racial confines of the early church in Acts.

The expansion was always at the Holy Spirit's initiative **vertically**. The Great Commission in Acts teaches us to observe the cross-cultural mission **horizontally** for which the Holy Spirit authorizes and empowers the people of God.

The Relational Paradigm in Great Commandment

Jesus Christ came to the World not to abolish the law, rather, to fulfill the law. The law in the Old Testament is summarized in two: "Love the Lord your God with all your heart and with all your soul and with all your strength and with all your mind and, love your neighbor as yourself" (Luke 10:27). Jesus, quoting from Leviticus 19:18, commented, "the second and Great Commandment" (second in

---

[31] Yoder, 84-85.
[32] Yoder, 87.

importance only to the supreme commandment to love God with all our being), and elaborated on it in the Sermon on the Mount. Mary's sitting at the feet of Jesus and the compassionate good Samaritan reflect **the vertical and horizontal aspects** respectively in Christian witness (Luke 10). The holistic mission demands word and deed in witness. In God's perspective, neighbor includes the one in need. The relation between the Great Commission and the Great Commandment is debated among the people. Some consider them as identical so that if the Gospel is shared with others, the Great Commandment is also completed. John Stott denies this and says that,

> the Great commission neither explains, nor exhausts, nor supersedes the Great commandment. If we love our neighbor, we must inevitably be concerned for their total welfare, the good of their soul, their body and their community. We should be concerned with preventive medicine or community health as well, which means the quest for better social structures in which peace, dignity, freedom, and justice are secured for all. There is no reason why, in pursuing this quest, we should not join hands with all people of good will, even if they are not questions.[33]

We are sent into the World to be the salt of the earth and the light of the World **horizontally** (Matt. 5:13-16). The Church is a worshipping as well as a serving community, and although worship and service belong together they are not to be confused. Christians need to gain a healthy perspective for a **holistic witness** in a community where values are deteriorated. John Stott brings the broader vision for Christian mission from a biblical synthesis,

> Jesus Christ calls all His disciples to "ministry," that is, to service. He Himself is the servant *par excellence*, and He calls us to be servants too. This much then is certain: if we are Christians, we must spend our lives in the service of God and others. The only difference between us lies in the nature of the service we are called to render. Some are called to be missionaries, evangelists, or pastors, and others to the great professions of law, education, medicine, and the social sciences. But others are called to commerce, to industry and farming, to accountancy and banking, to local government or Parliament, and to the mass media, to home making and family building...but as their Christian vocation, as the way Christ has called them to spend their lives in His service. Further, a part of their calling will be to seek to maintain Christ's standards of justice, righteousness, honesty, human dignity, and compassion in a society that no longer accepts them.[34]

The new commandment by Jesus, "love one another; as I have loved you, so you are to love one another" (John.13:34) is revolutionary in nature. "It's new in kind, meant a transformed kind of life, qualitatively new in its outward, sacrificial, self-giving sense."[35] It is only in the context of loving God **(vertical)** and loving others **(horizontal)** that the Church has life at all. Our proclaiming witness or yearnings for numerical growth are meaningless outside the light of this supreme mark, "love one another" (*koinonia*); if not, we would fall into the unhealthy situation Peter Wagner calls *koinonitis* (hyper-cooperativism). "Fellowship, by definition involves inter-personal relationships. It happens when Christian believers get to know one another, enjoy one another, and to care for one another. But

---

[33] John R W Stott and Christopher Wright, *Christian Mission in the Modern World*, (Downers Grove: IVP Books, 1975, 2015), 29.
[34] Stott and Wright, 31.
[35] Charles Van Engen, *Growth of the True Church*, (Amsterdam: Rodopi, 1981), 167.

as the disease develops, *koinonia* becomes *koinonitis."*[36] Christians need to develop healthy fellowship in community (Acts 2:42, Phil. 1:5, 1 John 1:7).

Human Responses in Deliverance Ministry

In reference to human responses in deliverance ministry, we come across people who fall during prayer or break out laughing hysterically. It has become common in revival meetings throughout history. People may run, leap, shout, cry, sit in silence, fall, laugh, or respond with other such demonstrations. Thomas E Trask analyzed the developments in such situations and held a healthy perspective:

> People sometimes say that "God is doing a new thing." There is a strong tendency to try to establish the spiritual authenticity of these behaviors by asserting that God is making people act in a certain way, that "God made me do it." This is usually not the case, nor is proof of divine initiative necessary to affirm the spiritual authenticity of these experiences. In many situations, people are simply responding to a new awareness of the presence of God, doing so in a way that suits their personality, culture, and group expectations at the time. People act in ways that are new to them during revival; this doesn't mean that God makes them to do whatever they are doing. When David saw the ark coming, he danced before the Lord. God did not make David dance. People are personally involved in these human responses.[37]

---

[36] Peter C Wagner, *Your Church Can Be Healthy,* (Nashville: Abingdon Press, 1979), 78.
[37] Thomas E Trask, "Signs and Wonders," in Thomas E Trask, Zenas J Bicket, and Wayde I Goodall (eds), *The Pentecostal Pastor: A Mandate for the 21st Century,* (Springfield, MO: Gospel Publishing House, 2003) 308-309.

Trinity

Theme	Father	Son	Holy Spirit
Gracious Call	Discipleship (Mt. 28:19-20)	Discipleship (Mt. 28:19-20)	Discipleship (Mt. 28:19-20)
Great Commission	Witness (Isa. 46.9)	Witness (Acts 1:8)	Witness (Acts 13:1-3, 20:23)
Great Commandment	Servant (Jam. 1:1)	Servant (Rom. 1:2)	Servant (Luke 4:19)
Glorious Gifts	Steward (1 Cor. 1:21)	Steward (Eph. 4:11-12)	Steward (Rom. 12:4-5, 1 Cor. 12:4-7)
Glorious Ministry	Ambassador (2 Cor. 5:18-19, Rom. 5:5-10)	Ambassador (Col. 1:19-22, Eph. 2:15-16)	Ambassador (Acts 15:28, Eph. 4:3-7)

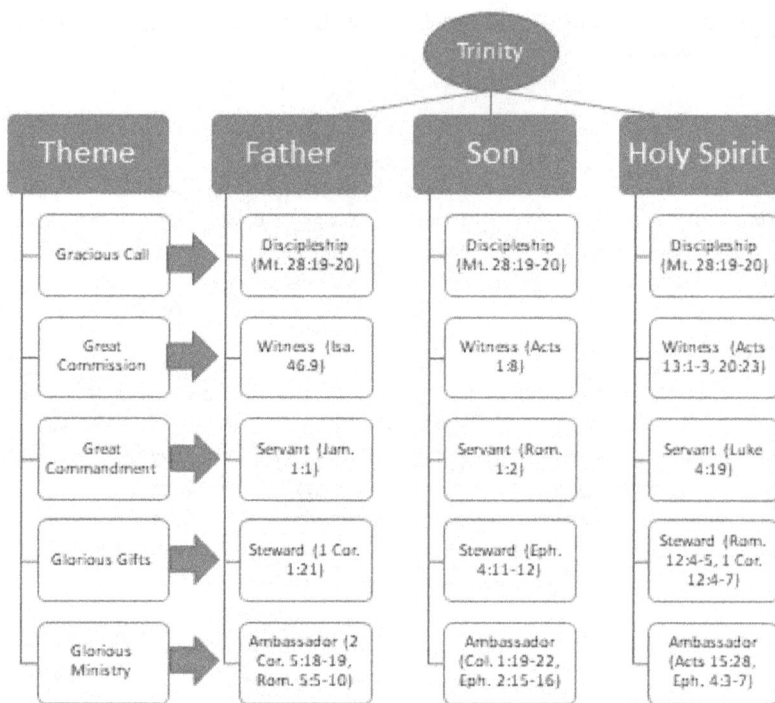

Figure 2: A Relational Paradigm in Theology of Mission

Proclamation: The Gospel of Grace

There are several passages in the Old Testament which emphasize the saving grace of God over against the sin and failure of humanity (Gen. 3:15, 9:27, 12:1-3). The core of Christian mission, what David Bosch calls "the heart" of Mission, is evangelism: giving witness to the Gospel. The Gospel that Paul mentioned is tied to the broader story of the mission of God (*missio Dei*). Christ died for our sins, was buried, and was raised on the third day – all built upon the foundation of the scriptures (1 Cor. 15:3-4). The four Gospels describe the link between the Testaments. Matthew started his Gospel by tracing the lineage of Jesus back to Abraham (Matt. 1:1) and identified Jesus as the very presence of God among men, the Immanuel (Matt. 1:23, Isa. 7:14). Luke's historical account traced Jesus' genealogy all the way back to God Himself (Luke 3:23-38), in addition to tying the birth of Jesus to several Old Testament promises (Luke 1:67-79). John's Gospel takes the story back into eternity past displaying Christ as Creator (John 1:1-3). Though the story of the Gospel cannot be told without the Old Testament context, the Christ-event is unique in salvation history. The Gospel is truly eternal and cosmic because the story of Jesus is eternal in scope and cosmic in its implications.

The Core of the Proclamation

"The noun 'Gospel' (*euangelion* – Gk) is used seventy-five times in the New Testament (fifty-eight times by Paul). As a verb to evangelize, preach, proclaim (*euangelizomai*) it is used fifty-three times (twenty by Paul)."[38] "The Gospel of grace" is centered on the meaning of the cross of Jesus Christ. Paul speaks of the Gospel as parallel to the message of the cross, "For Christ didn't send me to baptize, but to preach the Gospel, not with words of human wisdom, lest the cross of Christ be emptied of its power. For the message of the cross is foolishness to those perishing, but to us who are being saved it is the power of God" (1 Cor. 1:17-18). The core message of the Gospel is about the grace of God offered for all of humanity. When Peter was called to speak to Cornelius he summarized to the Jewish believers in Jerusalem, "God, Who knows the heart, showed that He accepted them by giving the Holy Spirit to them, just as He did to us. He didn't discriminate between us and them, for He purified their hearts by faith. Now, then, why do you try to test God by putting on the necks of the Gentiles a yoke that neither we nor our ancestors have been able to bear? No! We believe it is through the grace of our Lord Jesus Christ that we are saved, just as they are" (Acts 15:8-11). This experience, which required special visions of revelation for both Peter and Cornelius, prevented Christianity from becoming a Jewish sect. From first to last, it was the grace of God that saved all people: Jews who walked with Jesus, as well as Cornelius and his household. Grace plus nothing is the Gospel message. Paul also summarizes the core understanding of the Gospel before the Ephesian elders, "If only I may finish the race and complete the task the Lord Jesus has given me, the task of testifying to the Gospel of God's grace" (Acts 20:24).

In the Greek New Testament, the *kerygma* literally refers to the preaching. Jesus was sent out to preach good news to the poor and proclaim freedom to the captives. His proclaiming included recovery of sight to the blind, which was literally accomplished (Luke 7:21-22, 18:35-43). He was also sent to proclaim the year of God's favor. The first recorded preaching of Peter on the day of Pentecost was an evangelistic proclamation (Acts 2:17-40). Though he was very enthusiastic on several occasions, he had turned into a coward after Jesus' death. He was transformed on the day of Pentecost. Peter was baptized, filled, and anointed with the Holy Spirit as was promised by Jesus. "But you shall receive power when the Holy Spirit comes upon you (**vertical**); you shall be My witnesses in Jerusalem, and in Judea and Samaria, and to the end of the earth" (**horizontal**) (1:8). The word "power" (*dunamis* – Gk) indicates a dynamic enablement, or an ongoing source of power. O S Hawkins, in his article "Passionate proclamation: the eternal effects of evangelistic preaching," writes,

> Peter's Pentecost sermon provides many elements for us to understand about the proclamation of God's Word. It is Prophetic (Acts 2:17-21, 25-29, 34-35), Plain (2:22-23), Positive (2:24, 32), and Personal (2:22-23, 36). When these elements are present, the proclamation of God's Word should be penetrating and cut to the heart (2:37).[39]

---

[38] Scott W Sunquist, Understanding Christian Mission: Participation in Suffering and Glory, (Grand Rapids: Baker Academic, 2013), 215.

[39] O S Hawkins, "Passionate Proclamation: The Eternal Effects of Evangelistic Preaching," in Timothy Beougher and Alvin Reid (eds), *Evangelism for a Changing World: Essays in Honor of Roy J Fish*, (Wheaton: Harold Shaw Publishers, 1995), 130.

Proclamation of the Gospel should be at the center of the Church today. It's still by the foolishness of preaching that men and women are drawn to repentance (1 Cor. 1:23-24). The Word of God is alive and powerfully proclaimed and God brings conviction in human hearts. Whereas Jesus was empowered to proclaim the good news of the Kingdom, the Church is empowered to proclaim the Gospel of grace and reconciliation focusing on the Kingdom. The preaching ministry of the church invites people to respond to saving grace as the only entrance to the Kingdom of God. Murray Dempster, in the article "Evangelism, Social Concern, and the Kingdom of God," writes, "from an eschatological perspective, the mission of the Church is to witness to the truth that the Kingdom of God which still belongs to the future has already broken into the present age in Jesus Christ and continues in the world through the power of the Holy Spirit."[40] A B Simpson, the founder of the Alliance Movement in Canada and the USA which paved the way for such a powerful proclamation more than hundred years ago, said, "The fourfold Gospel: Jesus Christ is the Savior (Acts 4:12), Sanctifier (1 Cor. 1:30), Healer (James 5:15), and the soon coming King (Acts 1:11)."[41] It is the heartbeat of the Alliance people which was adopted by Pentecostals all over the World.

The Proclamation and Cultural Context

As communicators of God's Word, we need to be students of the World for effective presentation. Jesus always began where people were and spoke the truth people needed to hear, not what they wanted to hear. Roy Clements says, "Prophetic preaching is speaking God's truth to a specific place and time, digging into where people are and applying the Bible in specific ways to their circumstances. It's risky but it is a risk we need to take. We can't play it safe."[42]

Ed Stetzer and David Putman quote the words of Darrin Patrick in writing on the topic, "Breaking the code without compromising the Faith, God is true":

He has revealed Himself in two unique ways: in Jesus Who came and died and rose again in the flesh, and in His written Word, the Bible. Therefore, we will seek to know, live, and proclaim truth out of our love for God. Just as Jesus came into a specific context at a specific time, we also realize that our fellowship exists in a specific context at a specific time. Therefore, we will seek to proclaim truth in the context of cultures in which we are situated."[43]

Bruce Riley Ashford elucidates well on the proclamation of Gospel and culture in an appropriate contextualization in theological development:

We must proclaim and plant Churches in three ways: faithfully, meaningfully, and dialogically. We must pay careful attention to our beliefs and practices, ensuring that we express

---

[40] Murray A Dempster, "Evangelism, Social Concern, and the Kingdom of God," in Murray W Dempster, Byron D Klaus, and Douglas Petersen (eds), *Called & Empowered: Global Mission in Pentecostal Perspective,* (Peabody, MA: Hendrickson Publishers, 1991), 24.
[41] A B Simpson, "The Fourfold Gospel," https://www.cmalliance.org/about/beliefs/fourfold-Gospel (Accessed September 28, 2017).
[42] Roy Clements, quoted in David W Henderson, *Culture Shift: Communicating God's Truth in a Changing World,* (Grand Rapids: Baker Books, 1998), 44.
[43] Ed Stetzer and David Putman, *Breaking the Missional Code,* (Nashville: Broadman & Holman Publishers, 2006), 180.

and embody the gospel in cultural forms that are faithful to the scriptures, it is important to interpret scriptures accurately before proclaiming them within a cultural context.[44]

We want the hearers to understand the words we speak and the actions we perform in the way that we intend; we want them to be able to respond in a way that is meaningful in a particular context. David K Clark writes, "in taking a dialogical approach, the Christian who seeks to evangelize, plant Churches, disciple, or pastor within a particular context will find himself in a continued dialogue with that cultural context."[45] Paul's mission in Athens and his public proclamation at Mars Hill give us a model for proclamation among people who never had any association with Christianity. He engaged in dialogue with Jews and God-fearing Greeks in the synagogue and market places, and then in the public hall at Mars Hill with the philosophers. The significant lesson in it is the priority of listening to people, culture, and life situation in the proclamation of the message of the Gospel. Zac Niringiye, in the article "To proclaim the good news of the Kingdom," writes, "listening and dialogue are rooted in the conviction that every culture, era, or society has within it something equivalent to the 'unknown God' of the Athenians, which ought to be the starting point of the proclamation."[46] Paul commends the Athenians' sincere desire to worship the true God and not the material manifestations in the form of idols. It's true in the context of Asia and Africa where, sadly, missionaries engaged in proclaiming the Gospel do so with the attitude of condemnation rather than commendation.

Ken Gnanakan raised the challenge to review our attitude of presenting a radical discontinuity between one's present faith and the saving faith in Jesus Christ but advocated a realistic approach, "our proclamation must be based on the uniqueness of Biblical revelation of God in the Lord Jesus Christ but, related to our present world through the love of God demonstrated in Jesus."[47]

The Word of God has the power to convict of sin. We read in Acts 2:37: "Now when they heard this, they were cut to the heart, and said to Peter and the rest of the apostles, 'Men and brethren, what shall we do?'" It is the Holy Spirit Who pricked their minds and hearts *through* Peter's preaching the Word of God. Michael Green writes, "One of the great weaknesses in contemporary Christianity is the poverty of preaching. Many clergy consider it a chore, and many congregations complain if it lasts 10 minutes."[48]

The Spirit-Anointed Proclamation

The message becomes life changing (**vertical+horizontal**) only when it is prepared and proclaimed under the anointing of the Holy Spirit (**vertical**). The printed scripture becomes activated in the hearts of the hearers as the Word of God through the anointed preaching. In other words, written word (*logos*) needs to be elevated as spoken word for life transformation (**vertical+horizontal**). The anointing (**vertical**) makes the difference in the proclamation of an anointed preacher. Ernest Moen, in the article "Pentecostal Preaching," writes, "His words are divinely inspired, easy to understand, powerful in context."[49] The book of Acts is full of examples of preaching

[44] Ashford, "The Gospel and Culture," in *Theology and Practice of Mission*, 120.
[45] David K Clark, *To Know and Love God*, (Wheaton: Crossway, 2003), 115.
[46] Zac Niringiye, "To Proclaim the Good News of the Kingdom," in Andrew Walls and Cathy Ross, *Mission in the 21st Century*, (Maryknoll, NY: Orbis Books, 2008), 23.
[47] Ken Gnanakan, "To Proclaim the Good News of the Kingdom," in Walls and Ross, 10.
[48] Michael Green, *I Believe in The Holy Spirit*, (Grand Rapids: William B Eerdmans Publishing, 1975), 134.
[49] Ernest J Moen, "Pentecostal Preaching," in Trask, Bicket, and Goodall (eds), 591.

followed by Spirit-initiated results. Three thousand, in Acts 2, repented from sins and were baptized in water as an outward expression of inward faith. In Acts 4, five thousand believed in the Gospel. Acts 6 indicates the number of disciples multiplied...and a great company of the priests were obedient to the faith. According to Acts 9:35, all who dwelt in Lydda and Sharon...turned to the Lord. A great number believed, in Acts 11:21, and turned to the Lord. In Acts 13:44, almost the whole city gathered to hear the Word of God. The early disciples proclaimed the Gospel (**vertical+horizontal**) with the anointing of the Holy Spirit (**vertical**). It resulted in large numbers of people becoming the disciples of Christ and the churches were strengthened in faith (14:21-22, 16:5). Paul and Silas were identified with those who have turned the World upside down (17:6). When the Gospel was preached in Ephesus, the Word of the Lord grew mightily and prevailed (19:20). The Spirit-anointed proclamation made a difference in their witness.

Acts of the Apostles emphasizes three points concerning Spirit-guided witness, a result of Spirit-anointing. First, the person of Jesus Christ: Especially His suffering, death and resurrection, proclaiming the good news about Jesus (Acts 8:35, cf. 5:42, 28:31). Second, the gift of God to humanity: Different words are used to describe the meaning of Jesus' life and ministry: forgiveness, eternal life, grace, reconciliation, peace, and salvation. Forgiveness of sins and the Holy Spirit get special attention in Acts (2:38, 9:17-18, 22:16). Third, the invitation to accept the call of God: A human decision to accept the call of God means repentance toward God and faith toward our Lord Jesus (20:21) with baptism as a sign of the new life and the incorporation into a new community (2:37-41).

These three essential parts of the witness, as described in Acts, are clearly expressed in Peter's sermon after Pentecost. In Peter's sermon the Word is added to the Spirit, the Word explains the event of the descending of the Spirit. For Peter, Pentecost is the fulfillment of the prophesy of Joel about the pouring out of the Spirit of God, in the last days, upon all flesh. The close connection between Spirit and witness is stressed by Peter in addition made to the text of Joel; the words "and they shall prophesy" are added to the text (Acts 2:18).[50]

Christian conversion and regeneration (**vertical+horizontal**) remain miracles of God's grace (**vertical**). There is power in the proclamation of the Gospel. Apostle Paul portrays the god of this World as having blinded the minds of unbelievers, to keep them from seeing the light of the Gospel of the glory of Christ (2 Cor. 4:4). Preaching the Gospel is the God-appointed means by which the prince of darkness gets defeated and the light comes streaming into people's hearts. There is power in the Gospel of grace for salvation-enabled people to see the reconciliatory work of Jesus Christ on the cross. Paul says that it is his passion to make Christ known (Rom. 15:20-21). It began for him with a revelation of Jesus Christ (Gal. 2:2). He not only encountered Christ on the Road to Damascus, he kept on meeting Jesus every day with enlightened eyes of the heart (Eph. 1:18). This revelation of Jesus, and Paul's study of God's purposes, gave birth to his apostolic passion. It was so focused that the Gentiles might become an offering acceptable to God, sanctified by the Holy Spirit (Rom. 15:16). Paul's ministry is presented as an accomplishment of Christ for obedience to God in the power of the Spirit (17-19a). Due to that fact, glory is to be given to God alone. Here, Paul sees himself as nothing but an agent of an active Triune God Who is really the One Who has the initiative. He also acknowledges the

---

[50] Wilbert R Shenk (ed), The Transfiguration of Mission: Biblical, Theological, and Historical Foundations, (Scottdale, PA: Herald Press, 1993), 116.

particular calls for others and the complementarity of tasks within a holistic view of mission (1 Cor. 3:5-15). Samuel Escobar writes, "Paul doesn't need to use marketing techniques to prove that his own call is the best and the most urgent in order to attract donors from competing agencies."[51]

In his article, "Apostolic Passion: Human enthusiasm cannot sustain apostolic passion," Floyd McClung writes, "when God invests His passion in you – the desire to see His name glorified among all people – you must build and develop what God has given you."[52] Billy Graham, who touched millions of lives through the proclamation of the Gospel, found the power of the Gospel inherent within the Word of God itself. So assured of what he had been doing even after 50 years in ministry, he defined, "an evangelist is a person who has been called and especially equipped by God to declare the good news to those who have not yet accepted it, with the goal of challenging them to turn to Christ in repentance and faith and to follow Him in obedience to His will."[53] Preaching is one of the means of communicating God's truth to persons through a person. Philip Brooks, who declared his confidence in the power of God to change persons through preaching the good news, said, "the neglect of Biblical preaching weakens the witness of the church because it violates the biblical image of the ministry."[54]

It was through Spirit-anointed preaching that the church was planted in the pagan World and was renewed in the 16th century. The centrality of the proclamation of the Gospel as part of the holistic approach to Mission is to be upheld everywhere. As Orlando Costas writes, "If present-day Christianity is not to be reduced to a Museum piece, a historically insignificant religion, a topic of the past, a corpse or a free-floating religious club, it will need to recover the urgency of proclaiming three things: the name of Jesus, the radical nature of God's Kingdom, and the call to repentance and faith."[55] Evangelical Christians have always emphasized the necessity of preaching the Gospel, for God has appointed His Church to be the herald of the good news. John Stott quotes the extreme view of D Martyn Lloyd-Jones who emphasized the primacy of preaching:

To me the work of preaching is the highest and the greatest and the most glorious calling to which anyone can ever be called. If you want something in addition to that I would say without any hesitation that the most urgent need in the Christian Church today is true preaching, and as it is the greatest and most urgent need in the Church, it is obviously the greatest need for the world also.[56]

Practice: Christian Discipleship

Matthew 28:18-20, often quoted as the Great Commission of Jesus Christ, highlights the theme of discipleship. Here, the divine priority given to teaching makes discipleship imperative for all who

---

[51] Samuel Escobar, in Charles Van Engen, Dean S Gilliland, and Paul Pierson (eds), *The Good News of the Kingdom*, Congratulatory ed., (Maryknoll: Orbis Books, 1993), 59.

[52] Floyd McClung, "Apostolic Passion: Human Enthusiasm Cannot Sustain Apostolic Passion," in Winter and Hawthorne (eds), 186.

[53] Billy Graham, *Just as I Am: The Autobiography of Billy Graham,* (New York: Harper Collins, 2007), xvii.

[54] Philip Brooks, in Lloyd M Perry and Norman Shawchuck, *Revitalizing the Twentieth Century Church,* (Chicago, Moody Press, 1982), 113-14.

[55] Orlando Costas, The Integrity of Mission: The Inner Life and Outreach of the Church, (San Francisco: Harper and Row, 1979), 12.

[56] D Martyn Lloyd-Jones, in Stott and Wright, 97.

respond to the proclamation of the Gospel. Paul was aware of the divine authority behind the Gospel and declared it to the church at Galatia, "I want you to know, brothers, that the Gospel I preached is not something that man made up. I received it by revelation from Jesus Christ" (Gal. 1:11-12).

Meaning of the term "disciple"

The term "disciple" (*mathetes*) is used 37 times in Luke and 28 times in Acts of the Apostles. Most of the scenes in Acts involve texts where the term "disciples" serves as another name for "believers."[57] The words "make disciples of all nations" (*panta ta ethne*) are crucial for understanding the missionary task of the church. It's a reference to all the ethnic groups (people groups). Christ's desire for all the people was evident in His words, "then He opened their minds to understand the scriptures and said to them, 'thus it is written, that Christ should suffer and on the third day rise from the dead, and that repentance and forgiveness of sins should be preached in His name to all nations beginning from Jerusalem'" (Luke 24:45-47). The phrase *panta ta ethne* occurs in the Greek Old Testament some 100 times and virtually never carries the meaning of Gentile individuals but always carries the meaning "all the nations" in the sense of people groups outside Israel."[58]

The Great Commission is clearly a Kingdom commission. Jesus issued His orders after assuring His disciples that He had received all authority and power in heaven and on earth. The task of mission was not confined to the twelve. It is a fact in understanding the conception of evangelism and discipleship. Luke is the only Gospel author to record a further mission by seventy other disciples which is significant, for it serves to highlight his strong interest in missions and evangelism. What is addressed to the twelve in Matthew (cf. Matt. 10:7-16ff, 11:21-23) is addressed to the seventy in Luke (10:1-17). The marching orders involve nothing less than bringing the nations under the rule of the Word of Christ. So, the Kingdom mission is not limited to the few, rather is the continuing work of the Church.

The Witness in Baptism

Jesus did not tell His followers to make disciples by gaining decisions or making converts, rather, make disciples. First, by baptism in the name of the Father, and of the Son, and of the Holy Spirit (Matt. 28:18-19). On the day of Pentecost, Peter's Spirit- anointed message challenged the hearts of the hearers which resulted in raising a question to know regarding the next step in their life. Repentance is a prerequisite for baptism and around 3000 were baptized on that day to follow Jesus Christ. Before baptizing the Ethiopian Eunuch, Philip asked if he truly believed in Jesus from the heart (Acts 8:37). Before baptizing the Jailor and his household, Paul and Silas explained the Gospel to him and his household (Acts 16:30-34).

Discipling the nations certainly involves calling people to make decision to turn to Christ in faith. Baptism is defined as an outward expression of our inward change. "It is a symbolic martyrdom and

[57] Darrel Bock and Andreas J Kostenberger (eds), *A Theology of Luke and Acts: Biblical Theology of the New Testament,* (Grand Rapids: Zondervan, 2012), 311.

[58] John Piper, "Discipling All the Peoples," in Winter and Hawthorne (eds), 115.

commits us to be martyrs, witnesses to the death of the things we have heard and seen."[59] In baptism, we are incorporated to Christ and to the church. An aspect of the sevenfold expression of the Church's unity (Eph. 4:4-6), baptism not only marks us as the Lord's possession, baptism also commits us to the other members of the body. Jesus prayed that the Church would display her unity before the World that the "world may know that You sent Me" (John 17:20-23). In a context where the church is deeply fragmented, the significance and meaning of baptism reminds us to focus on Christ-centered and Spirit-anointed witness. By baptism, those who turn to Christ in faith come under the shepherding love of Christ, exercised through the anointed ministers (Matt. 18:15-20, Heb. 13:17). Apostles preached good news and won a large number of disciples, strengthened them, and encouraged them to remain true to the faith in the first missionary journey. Paul and Barnabas appointed elders for them in each church and committed them to the Lord (Acts 14:21-23).

Teaching on Discipleship

The second tool for the discipling of the nations is teaching. The Apostles were commissioned to teach the nations everything that Jesus commanded. Preachers proclaim the Gospel of Christ, calling all to respond in faith and repentance. Going forward the community is to be taught all that Christ has commanded. The priority was set for leading a holy life in the corrupt generation (Acts 2:40). Suffering and hardships were counted as worthy to endure on the way to the Kingdom of God (Acts 14:22, 2 Thess. 1:5). In this way the nations become obedient worshippers and witnesses of God.

Jesus Christ has called us to make disciples and to teach them all that He has commanded us. We can only make disciples by engaging life to life, person to person. That's why the Lord Jesus walked and talked, ate and prayed, laughed and wept with His disciples. He made disciples by sharing His life with them. This is not optional work but mandatory. David M Sills writes in the article, "Mission and Discipleship,"

> Evangelizing without follow-up and discipleship is tantamount to having babies and leaving them on the side walk outside the hospital when we go home. There is a responsibility for the parents to raise their children in the fear and admonition of the Lord, and a similar responsibility falls on the missionaries. We best do this by modeling it in how we intentionally teach them, nurture their walk with the Lord, and mentor them in a life of ministry commitment.[60]

A disciple is one who has been reconciled unto God and experiences the inward transformation of regeneration by the Holy Spirit. It is the result of Spirit-anointed witness in the World. Peter Wagner goes beyond presence and proclamation in evangelism and affirms persuasion which insists on making disciples. In order to be counted as a disciple, a person should be committed not only to Jesus Christ, but also to the body of Christ.[61] Discipleship means adherence to Christ. Christianity without the living Christ is Christianity without discipleship.

Jesus also built in leadership among His disciples since He chose twelve from among them (Luke 6:13). The ethical core of love the disciples should have is recorded in Jesus' sermon (6:27-36). It

[59] Peter J Leithart, The Kingdom and the Power: Rediscovering the Centrality of the Church, (Phillipsburg, NJ: P&R Publishing, 1993), 189-90.
[60] David M Sills, "Mission and Discipleship," in Ashford (ed), 195-196.
[61]Peter Wagner, "On the Cutting Edge of the Missionary Strategy," in Winter and Hawthorne (eds), 532-33.

issues a call to love one's enemies which was attested through God's care for the unrighteous. No disciple is greater than his teacher, so the model of teaching matters (6:40).

The disciples witnessed Jesus' miraculous acts. They were with Him when He raised the widow of Nain's son (Luke 7:11-15). His actions in healing the blind, lame, deaf, and others are the evidence He gives to the question raised by John the Baptist. Jesus' power is displayed to the disciples when He calms the storm (Luke 8:22-25). Events like this make the disciples perceive Jesus' authority, an authority like God's ability to control the seas (Ps. 107:23-30).

The disciples learned from the Master (Luke 8:4-15). They asked Jesus to teach them about the parable of the sower. In the interpretation from Jesus, they learned that Satan grabs the Word before some have a chance, others have a short-lived faith but, persecution causes them to fall away, while the concerns and riches of life choke the Word in the lives of still others. "There are those who with an honest and good heart hold fast to the Word and bear fruit with patience. Disciples are to have the heart of the good soil."[62]

Prayer is viewed as integral in discipleship. They asked Jesus to teach them to pray. His model prayer includes affirmation of God's uniqueness, submission to His will, an acknowledgement of daily needs, and a prayer for spiritual protection (Luke 11:1-4). The disciples' prayer is intercession that communicated complete dependence on God in every key sphere of life.[63]

Discipleship is about service and suffering. They had to learn much regarding their role as disciples in various situations they confronted. They failed to exorcise a demon from a boy (Luke 9:40) and responded poorly to the rejection by some in Samaria; they wanted to bring judgement immediately rather than continuing to witness in the face of rejection (9:54-56). James and John wanted fire to rain down from heaven yet Jesus rebuked them while moving on with an anointed witness. Jesus was preparing them for service and suffering, as was in His life. A disciple is to take his cross daily and lose his life to gain it, not being ashamed of the Son of Man (Luke 9:23-27). He repeated the matter, "the Son of Man is going to be betrayed" (9:43b-44).

Luke narrates an account of three men who encountered Jesus (Luke. 9:57-62). The first one offers to follow Jesus without waiting to be called. The gulf between a voluntary offer to follow and genuine discipleship is clear in this encounter. His optimism in following Jesus without realizing the requirement of leaving everything behind, even home, was affirmed by Jesus in His words, "Foxes have holes and birds of the air have nests, but the Son of Man has no place to lay His head" (9:58). A disciple of Jesus must realize that following Jesus means living as a stranger in this World because a choice for Jesus is a choice rejected by many in the World. The second one heard the call from Jesus, but he wanted to bury his father before he started to follow. A definite legal ordinance acts as a barrier between Jesus and the man. Nothing on earth could be allowed to stand between Jesus and the man He has called. The call of Jesus is stronger than the barrier. Here, it is highly probable that the man is asking to wait until his father has passed away – whenever that would happen. He wanted to postpone following Jesus for an indefinite period. He wanted to put commitment to family ahead of service to the Kingdom of God (9:60). The priority should be set in Christian discipleship. The third person expresses his willingness to follow yet makes his own offer on his own terms. Discipleship can tolerate no conditions which might come between Jesus and our obedience to Him. Jesus denied the

---

[62] Bock and Kostenberger, 317.
[63] Bock and Kostenberger, 321.

opportunity of discipleship through the sharp words, "no man having put his hand to the plough and looking back is fit for the Kingdom of God" (Luke 9: 62). Israelites looked back after the exodus (Exod. 16:3). Lot's wife looked back after departing Sodom (Gen. 19:26, Luke 17:32). Demas deserted Paul and went to Thessalonica because he loved the World (2 Tim. 4:10). To follow Jesus means not to look back to the way of life in the past rather marching onward with the mandate of the Master.

Grace and Discipleship

On two separate occasions Peter received the call "follow Me." It was the first and last word Jesus spoke to His disciple (Mark 1:17, John 21:22). A whole life lies between these two calls. The first occasion was by the lake of Gennesaret, when Peter left his nets and his craft and followed Jesus at His word. The second occasion is when the risen Lord finds him back again at his old trade and met the urgent need with the task of restoration which results in Peter's confession. Each time, it is the same grace of Christ which calls him, "follow Me." The grace was not self-bestowed. It was the grace of Christ Himself, now prevailing upon himself to leave all and follow Him even to the extent of the supreme fellowship of martyrdom for his Lord. He had received the grace which costs. What does Jesus mean to us in different professions? Drawing on the Sermon on the Mount, Dietrich Bonhoeffer answers the question, providing a seminal reading of the dichotomy between cheap grace and costly grace:

> Cheap grace is the preaching of forgiveness without requiring repentance, baptism without church discipline, communion without confession, absolution without personal confession. Cheap grace is without discipleship. Grace without the cross, grace without Jesus Christ, living and incarnate Word.[64]

Christian discipleship is costly because it costs a man his life, and it is grace because it gives man the only true life. Bonhoeffer, as a young Lutheran Pastor, left the safety of America to return to Germany and became a martyr at the age of 39 in 1945. He had already made a monumental contribution to Christian thought. We live in a context that Christians are being persecuted all over the World. A true disciple of Christ confronts the challenges with courage and with commitment to follow Him to the last breath in life.

Discipleship to Jesus Christ was not like discipleship to a Jewish Rabbi. The rabbis bound their disciples not to themselves but to the Torah; Jesus bound His disciples to Himself. Jesus required His disciples to surrender without reservation to His authority. They thereby became not only disciples but also slaves (Luke 12:35ff, 42ff). This relationship has no parallel in Judaism.[65] Discipleship to Jesus meant complete personal commitment to Him and His message. The reason for this is the presence of the Kingdom in Jesus' person and message. Undivided loyalty is required in serving Jesus and the Kingdom.

Christian discipleship involves carrying one's cross in life (14:27). Counting the cost is a picture Jesus uses to describe discipleship in Luke 14:28-30. Before building, a wise man assesses the expense along with the benefits. It should be so with Christian discipleship. Discipleship also includes a

---

[64] Dietrich Bonhoeffer, *The Cost of Discipleship*, (New York: Touchstone, 1995), 44-45.
[65] George Eldon Ladd, *A Theology of the New Testament* (Grand Rapids: William B Eerdmans Publications, 1974), 108.

renunciation of possessions with a healthy perspective that God is more important than what we possess (14:33).

The lifelong journey of discipleship is the foundation for the pattern of Christian life in Acts: Those who accepted Peter's message were baptized, and about three thousand were added to their number that day. They devoted themselves to the apostles' teaching, and to fellowship, to the breaking of bread, and to prayer (2:42). This combination of faithfulness and a willingness to be instructed is what made the disciples so dynamic in Acts. All that Jesus taught the disciples they passed on faithfully to others. The result is that the church grows as it continues to be faithful in discipleship. Lesslie Newbigin writes,

> How is it possible that the Gospel should be credible, that people should come to believe that the power which has the last word in human affairs is represented by a Man hanging on the cross? I am suggesting that the only answer, the only hermeneutic of the Gospel, is a congregation of men and women who believe it and live by it.[66]

Christian life is to be lived in community. Discipleship was never intended to be a solo pursuit. Even as there is community within the Godhead, human beings are designed for relationship with others. It is in community that we experience and express love, forgiveness, compassion, justice, nurture, growth, and a host of other characteristics. It's God's intention that we should interact in families, tribes, and other social groups to display the life of Christ. Christian discipleship should flourish only in a context of commitment to love others. Jesus said, "A new commandment I give you: love one another. By this all men will know that you are My disciples, if you love one another" (John 13:34-35). God's people should minister to one another, encourage one another, press on to know and love God more deeply, and bring a variety of gifts and temperaments together to enrich one another. "Living in community, as the evidence of true discipleship, will model justice and mercy, compassion and forgiveness, love and joy, grace and generosity. None of these Christian fundamentals is possible without relationships."[67]

The vision of the church should be to influence youngsters to become disciples of Jesus Christ. Every Church needs trained adults to have a Jesus-focused ministry in an environment of prayer. It's an environment of grace as opposed to an environment of legalism. Following Jesus is better than keeping a bunch of rules. Why do young people wander away from youth ministry? One reason is they have external motivation, the values of their parents and the Church, yet have never internalized those values. How much better, in the context of discipleship, if we first say to them, "what do you believe God wants you to do?" The Holy Spirit works in their hearts and makes their character stronger because they are internally motivated rather than externally motivated. Secondly, we need to have a discipling ministry centered in relationships. We cannot disciple young people without having personal relationships. Third, we help young people reflect the character of Christ. We teach them the Bible, train them in the disciplines of the Christian life, show them how to have a quiet time, how to witness, and how to worship. Fourth, is the principle of reality. Discipleship takes place in real-life situations.

---

[66] Lesslie Newbigin, in Rose Dowsett, *The Great Commission*, (Mill Hill, London and Grand Rapids: Monarch Books, 2001), 52.
[67] Dowsett, 57.

Living as a royal priesthood, is a characteristic of disciples. Peter writes to a group of younger churches in the first century, "... you are a chosen people, a royal priesthood, a holy nation, a people belonging to God, that you may declare the praises of Him Who called you out of darkness into His wonderful light" (1 Pet. 2:9). God's people are called to represent God to people and people to God. Discipleship is a way of life, with the saving death of the Lord Jesus Christ at its heart.

Living in the light of Christ's return is very significant for the disciples. We are to live here-and-now yet at the same time in expectant faith looking for the Lord's return. This will change one's life, values, and priorities. In some parts of the World, Christians suffer greatly at the hands of hostile forces. From the very beginning of the Church, there have been martyrs for Christ. Paul wrote to the Church at Philippi, "I want to know Christ and the power of His resurrection and the fellowship of sharing in His sufferings, becoming like Him in His death, and so, somehow, to attain resurrection from the dead." If we walk the way of authentic discipleship, though, it will be costly as well as glorious.

There are many trends in the churches that attract a large number of people. When some come in and rather quickly express a commitment to Christ, they seemed to disappear equally as quickly. Discipleship in certain contexts began long before conversion, and conversion is simply part of the discipleship process.

Discipleship involves participation in community prior to conversion. Churches that facilitate this journey will recognize the importance of relationships, the currency that moves the unreached/unchurched forward. It is the need to make authentic relationships by the believers of the Church to find ways to engage them. Small group ministries will more and more reflect the culture of worship gatherings that are inviting to large numbers of unreached/unchurched people.[68]

Christian discipleship is for spiritual edification. It represents the educational purpose of the church. We must not only reach people, we must also teach people for spiritual maturity. Paul writes, "the body of Christ may be built up until we all reach unity in the faith and in the knowledge of the Son of God and become mature, attaining to the whole measure of the fullness of Christ" (Eph. 4:12b-13).

Demonstration: Power of God's Kingdom in Deliverance

The theme "God's Kingdom" was central in Jesus' mission. His mighty works were intended to prove that God's Kingdom had come upon them (Matt. 12:28). Jesus' teaching on "the Kingdom" was illustrated through different parables (Matt. 13:11-13). When the Word refers to God's Kingdom, it always refers to His reign, His rule, His sovereignty, and not to the realm in which it is exercised. The prayer taught by Jesus "Thy kingdom come; Thy will be done on earth as it is in heaven" is significant to understand the truth. George Eldon Ladd, in the article "The Gospel of the Kingdom," writes, "this prayer is a petition for God to reign, to manifest His kingly sovereignty and power, to put to flight

---

[68] Stetzer and Putman, 105.

every enemy of righteousness and of His divine rule that God alone may be King over all the world."
[69]

Paul writes, "For the Kingdom of God is not a matter of talk but of power" (1 Cor. 4:20). Jesus not only preached the Gospel of the Kingdom, He also demonstrated its power and His kingly compassion through the miracles He performed. He sent the apostles to preach the "Kingdom of God" and gave them power to heal and cast out demons (Luke 9:1-2). The church in the New Testament is commissioned with the equipping power of the Holy Spirit to exalt Jesus Christ and to demonstrate the power of the Kingdom. Peter Kuzmic, in the article "The Church and the Kingdom of God," writes,

> In the theological thinking of the past, Christology has been considered the basis for ecclesiology. The connection of the two was often seen in ontological terms which has not infrequently led to a very static view of the Church. Such a view was further fostered by institutionalization of the Church whose sole concerns were its own doctrine, order of worship, and self-serving organizational structures. The powerlessness and sterility of such churches became evident as soon as they lost the support of worldly powers and had to stand on their own. Such negative developments, along with the more positive recent Pentecostal- Charismatic renewal, led to an increasing recognition that the doctrine of the church also be founded on Pneumatology.[70]

Churches centered on institutionalism, sacramentalism, and legalism do not demonstrate the power of the Kingdom. Edgar R Lee brings a strong foundation for a charismatic presence while Christians are enabled to live in the presence of God. He writes in the article, "Living in the Presence of God: A Theology of Spiritual Formation,"

> In the New Testament, while the Holy Spirit may work sovereignly apart from any human instrumentality, the Spirit is usually transmitted through the Church by means of the gifts of the Spirit. After Pentecost, believers found themselves in a Church, newly equipped with a full range of spiritual gifts enabling both the twelve and others to do extra-ordinary things in their witness for Christ. They provided wise leadership (Acts 6:1-6), delivered inspired and potential sermons and public apologies (Acts 4:8ff, 6:10), worked dramatic healings (Acts 8:7, 14:8-10), gave accurate prophecies about the future (Acts 20:23, 21:4, 10, 11), and performed many signs and wonders (Acts 2:43, 5:12-16, 6:8, 8:6, 13, 19:11-12). The ministry of the Church may be charismatic, since it relates on the charismata, the gifts of the Spirit.[71]

The argument of Lesslie Newbigin is relevant including the Pentecostal emphasis on the role of the life-giving Spirit of God along with the apostolic witness (the emphasis of Protestantism), and true order, i.e. continuation of the apostolate (as stressed in Catholicism). He illustrates his criticism of the distortion and deficiency of the two views (Protestant and Catholic) by contrasting scriptural and church traditional criteria and practice: "The apostle asked the converts of Apollos one question, 'did

---

[69] George Eldon Ladd, "The Gospel of the Kingdom," in Winter and Hawthorne (eds), 66.

[70] Peter Kuzmic, "The Church and the Kingdom of God," in Daniel K Darko and Beth Snodderly (eds), *First the Kingdom of God: Global Voices on Global Mission,* (Pasadena, CA: William Carey International University Press, 2014), 34.

[71] Edgar R Lee, "Living in the Presence of God: A Theology of Spiritual Formation," *Enrichment Journal*, Summer 2002, http:/enrichmentjournal.ag.org/200203/200203_086_sptformation.cfm (Accessed September 10, 2017).

you receive the Holy Spirit when you believed?' His modern successors are more inclined to ask either 'did you believe exactly what we teach?' or 'were the hands that were laid on you our hands?' and if the answer is satisfactory – to assure the converts that they have received the Holy Spirit even if they don't know it. There is a world of difference between the two attitudes."[72] The experience in receiving the anointing of the Holy Spirit as the gift is different from the indwelling of the Holy Spirit, Who is in us forever from conversion.

Healing and Casting Out Demons

Jesus Christ commissioned the disciples to go through the villages of Israel, healing the sick, casting out demons, along with preaching the Gospel of the Kingdom of God (Luke 9:1-2, Matt. 10:1, Mark 3:14-15). Jesus tied together the ministries of healing, exorcism, and preaching the Gospel. K P Yohannan writes, "Jesus was routinely acknowledged as Lord by evil spirits, and He taught His disciples to take authority over them as He did."[73] We find the proclamation of the Gospel as integral in our mission, the accompanying signs and wonders cannot be neglected. The early disciples went out, preached everywhere after the ascension of Christ, the Lord worked with them, and confirmed the word by the signs that accompanied it (Mark 16:19-20). Salvation in the name of Jesus Christ is confirmed and testified by signs, wonders, and various miracles, and gifts of the Holy Spirit distributed according to the will of God (Heb. 2:3-4).

Although signs and wonders occur today, there are opinions that the supernatural work of the Spirit, sign gifts, ceased after the first century. The cessationist position holds that there are no signs and wonders today; signs and wonders occurred only in the First Century to establish the Church. These argue that Paul had this in mind in his writing of 1 Corinthians 13:8-10. They claim that Paul is here contending that the gifts of the Spirit would cease "when that which is perfect come." The cessationists consider "that which is perfect" as the scripture and when the Scriptures were completed at the end of the First Century, the gifts were no longer needed and ceased to function. However, we suggest that their position is in error on both scriptural and historical points of view. God provided for supernatural ministry by giving His Son, the Spirit, and Supernatural power, and this has not changed. First Corinthians clearly asserts that supernatural gifts are given to the Church until Christ, the Perfect One, comes again for the Church.

The history of Pentecostal, and now charismatic, mission carries thousands of stories of physical healings, deliverance from chemical addictions, exorcisms, and other extraordinary happenings that have changed the lives of people.

Signs, Wonders, and Demonic Deception

The Bible gives clear understanding that the devil will use miracles to deceive people and to lead them into apostasy and rejection of God (Matt. 7:21-23, 24:24, John 4:48, 1 Cor. 1:22-23, 2 Thess. 2:2-12, 1 Tim. 4:1, 2 Tim. 4:2-4, 2 Pet. 2:1-2, Rev. 13:13-14). Miracles alone are not proof that power comes

[72] Lesslie Newbigin, *The Household of God,* (London: SCM Press, 1953), 104.
[73] K P Yohannan, Why the World Waits: Exposing the Reality of Modern Missions, (Lake Mary, FL: Creations House, 1991), 95.

from God. It may come from the devil too. Miraculous ministry must be accompanied by sound doctrine. The ability to do miracles does not exempt a person from doctrinal evaluation.[74]

Spiritual Warfare

Jesus introduced God's Kingdom into the present World. This was a direct confrontation or invasion of the Kingdom of darkness ruled by Satan who is called the god of this age (2 Cor. 4:4). The topic of spiritual warfare has become a relevant topic in the area of missions, unlike in the past. Scott Moreau defined it as "the struggle that Christians have to live faithful Christian lives in the face of onslaughts of spiritual powers of darkness."[75] A belief in the ongoing activity of Spirits is prevalent in many parts of the World. Much discussion has taken place over several decades about the extent which a Christian can be influenced (demonized or possessed) by demons. However, Christians are asked to humble themselves before God, to be on guard that they would resist Satan (1 Pet. 5:8-9), and stand firm to face his attacks (Eph. 6:10-19). The warning and exhortation make it clear that Christians are not immune to his assaults.

Charles Kraft has contributed on the relevant subject "power encounter" and made a great impact on those engaged in deliverance ministry. Anthony Casey analyses the shift in Kraft's life as very interesting:

> First, Kraft's conversion and theological training pushed Kraft away from any openness to power Christianity. Second, Kraft's anthropological background gave him a framework for analyzing what was happening in his life as he began considering the reality of power Christianity. Third, Kraft's encounter with powerless Christianity compared to his encounters with power Christianity at Fuller Seminary further challenged his worldview. Finally, Kraft moved into what he describes as the third wave movement of the Holy Spirit within Evangelicalism.[76]

John Wimber's class at Fuller Theological Seminary, Pasadena, California, brought sharper focus to Kraft's understanding of spiritual power. He "moved into what he describes as the third wave movement of the Holy Spirit within Evangelicalism." Third wavers believe in the filling of the Holy Spirit for additional power to minister effectively. Kraft felt an immediate increase in his ability to minister and began speaking in tongues three or four years after being filled with the Spirit.[77] Without this additional filling the minister may be ineffective to command demons to leave. The Spirit-filling is to be a continuous experience of a Christian minister throughout life. Kraft challenged those who claim Christians cannot be demonized. He writes "all of us who deal with demonization, however, soon discover that we have to evict demons out of Christians."[78] Kraft describes inner healing as restoring of healthy relationships in three key areas: Our relationship with God helps us see ourselves as new and growing creatures. Our relationship with our self helps us understand how to accept, love,

---

[74] Gordon L Anderson, "Signs and Wonders," in Trask, Bicket, and Goodall (eds), 308.
[75] Scott A Moreau, Gary R Corwin, Gary B McGee (eds), *Introducing World Missions: A Biblical, Historical, and Practical Survey*, (Grand Rapids: Baker Academic, 2004), 288.
[76] Anthony Casey, *A New Reality: Charles Kraft's View of Spiritual Warfare* https://culturncity.files.wordpress.com/2011/04/kraft-on-spiritual-warfare.pdf (Accessed December 10, 2017).
[77] Charles Kraft, Christianity with Power: Your Worldview and Your Experience of the Supernatural, (Ann Arbor: Servant Books, 1989), 168.
[78] Charles Kraft, Confronting Powerless Christianity: Evangelicals and the Missing Dimension, (Grand Rapids: Chosen Books, 2002), 58.

and forgive our self as God does. Finally, our relationships with others help us accept, love, and forgive others as God does.[79] Power encounters contribute a different dimension to Christian experience. They focus on freedom from the enemy's activity. Satan is the blinder, restrictor, hinderer, crippler – the enemy who attempts to keep people from allegiance to God and truth. Peter Wagner, strong proponent of strategic-level spiritual warfare, writes, "the era between the first and second coming of Christ is an era of warfare between the two Kingdoms. Two powers are occupying the same territory."[80] People need freedom from the enemy to open their minds to receive and understand truth (2 Cor. 4:4) to release their will so that they can commit themselves to God. Jesus told the disciples to wait for spiritual power before they embarked on witness (Luke 24:49, Acts 1:4) just as Jesus Himself had waited to be empowered in His own baptism (Luke 3:21-22). Charles Kraft writes, "We are not fully equipped to witness without the freedom-bringing-truth-revealing power of the Holy Spirit."[81]

The proclamation of God's Kingdom always induces confrontation of forces. This phenomenon is very common in the Bible. In the Old Testament a power encounter is an important phenomenon (Gen. 3:1-5, 6:1-4, Deut. 4:19: 17:2-7: 1 Sam. 5:6: Dan. 10:13, 20). The story of the Ark of the Covenant among the Philistines is a clear illustration of the confrontation between YHWH and the false gods of the Philistines. The Philistines captured the Ark from Israel and placed it beside Dagon. The people of Ashdod found the next morning that Dagon had fallen face to the ground before the Ark of the Lord. They returned Dagon to place and the following morning found that it had fallen on its face again, with head and hands broken off and lying on the threshold. People of Ashdod and the neighboring town went through trouble and devastation. The same consequence was repeated in Gath and Ekron when the Ark was moved to those locations. Later Philistines realized that the power of the God of Israel surpassed the power of the gods of Philistia. So, they returned the Ark to Israel with a gift and sacrifice.

Likewise, Genesis 41:8 and 41:24 show that the power of God is far superior to that of the Egyptian Magicians, as God enables Joseph to interpret the King's dreams. God's power is proved greater, as the snake that came from Aaron's staff swallowed up the magician's staffs (Ex. 7:10-12). Daniel and his friends have ten times more wisdom and understanding than all the magicians and fortune tellers in the kingdom of Persia (Dan.1:20). No fortune teller, magician, sorcerer, astrologer, or wizard can explain the meaning of the King's dream, yet Daniel can, because God revealed the meaning to him. King Nebuchadnezzar realized that God is the greatest of all gods and the One Who reveals mysteries.

Early apostles in the first century confronted demonic powers revealed in the form of magic and occult. Simon the magician, seeing the gifts of the Holy Spirit, desires to buy the gift, even though he has been baptized. This shows that evil powers can still have hold of a believer (Acts 8:9-24). Bar-Jesus (Elymas) on Cyprus has magical powers and claims to be a prophet, yet he tries to stop the spreading of the Word. The Apostle Paul, filled with the power of the Holy Spirit, discerns the evil in him and brings about a temporary blindness on him (Acts 13:6-10). A slave girl could tell fortunes because of an evil spirit in her, and Paul cast out the demon from her (Acts 16:16-18). Newly

---

[79] Charles Kraft, Defeating Dark Angels: Breaking Demonic Oppression in the Believer's Life, (Ann Arbor: Servant Publications, 1992), 143.
[80] Peter C Wagner, "On the Cutting Edge of Mission Strategy," in Winter and Hawthorne (eds), 539.
[81] Charles Kraft, "Three Encounters in Christian Witness," in Winter and Hawthorne (eds), 412.

converted Christians who had practiced sorcery bring their scrolls and burn them publicly, indicating their complete renunciation of magic (Acts 19:19). The teaching in the New Testament is clear that those who practice witchcraft will not enter God's Kingdom (Gal. 5:20). Those who practice magic will be thrown into the lake of fire and Sulphur and will not be allowed to enter the city (Rev. 21:8, 22:15).

Spiritual warfare continues in the present age and increases, so that Christian congregations need more awareness of this reality. Satan blinds the eyes of the unbelievers (2 Cor. 4:4) and snatches the Word away when it is planted in their hearts (Luke 8:12). He gains physical control and oppresses (demonizes) people, bringing physical harm to those he thus affects (Luke 8:26-39, 9:37-43). He tempts (Acts 5:3, 1 Cor. 7:5, 1 Thess. 3:5), accuses and slanders (Rev. 12:10), discourages (1 Pet. 5:6-8), and persecutes (Rev. 2:10) believers. Spiritual warfare is both personal and corporate. Satan attacks churches, mission agencies, and church planting movements. He sows the seeds of doubt, mistrust, jealousy, anger, resentment, pride, and envy. He stimulates opposition from individuals, organizations, social structures, and governments. Harsh laws are made in certain countries in order to hinder people coming to Christ. Religious converts may be subjected to long periods of imprisonment in those countries. The government of India no longer issues visas to expatriate missionaries seeking to serve the Lord in that country.[82] We need a fresh anointing of the Holy Spirit to stand in opposition to the growing assaults of the enemy. E M Bounds said of the church and its leadership, "what the church needs today is not more machinery or better, not new organizations or more and novel methods, but men whom the Holy Ghost can use, men of prayer, men mighty in prayer... He does not anoint plans but men – men of prayer," quoted in Eastman's article "Developing a Prayer Ministry in the Church."[83] Jesus told His disciples if two of them agree on earth concerning anything that they ask it will be done for them by the Father in heaven (Matt. 18:19). As Paul Billheimer says, "the only power that overcomes Satan and releases souls from his stranglehold is the power of the Holy Spirit. The only power that releases the energy of the Spirit is the power of believing prayer" quoted in Eastman's article "Developing a Prayer Ministry in the Church." [84]

Enoch Wan, in "Spiritual Warfare: Understanding Demonization," writes,

> There are different types and stages of demonization: oppression, obsession, inhabitation, and possession. Oppression is the state/process of being tempted spiritually with a sense of being weighed down physically and psychologically. Possible symptoms are: heaviness or obstruction in body and/or mind; depression; discouragement; dullness; etc. Obsession is a persistent disturbing preoccupation with an often unreasonable and unnatural idea or feeling. Inhabitation is the process of being temporarily occupied, leading to being inhabited or indwelled by the devil or evil spirits (Luke 13:11-16, 1 Cor. 5:5). Possession is the act or state of being dominated or possessed by an extra-ordinary force (e.g. passion, impulse, idea) or extraneous personality (the devil or evil spirits). Demonic possession by evil spirits occurs among non-Christians who have not been born again and are subject to the complete control of Satan in the Kingdom of darkness.[85]

---

[82] Franklin Graham, "Missionary Evangelism," in Thom S Rainer (ed), *Evangelism in the Twenty-First Century*, (Wheaton: Harold Shaw Publishers, 1989), 164.
[83] Dick Eastman, "Developing a Prayer Ministry in the Church," in Trask, Bicket, and Goodall (eds), 247.
[84] Eastman, in Trask, Bicket, and Goodall (eds) 247.
[85] Enoch Wan, "Spiritual Warfare: Understanding Demonization," http://ojs.globalmissiology.org/index.php/english/article/view/443/1144 (Accessed December 05, 2017).

Spiritual warfare is a reality and the need of every Christian is to be aware of the spiritual equipment and the power to exercise spiritual authority over demonic power.

The Ministry of Deliverance

The key to the actual process of deliverance is authority. Demons are living beings who are serving their master Satan. Satan is the ruler of the World but, the position and power of Jesus is above all (Eph. 1:18-23). Jesus gave His disciples His power and authority to go and cast out demons (Gk: *ekballo*, meaning "to throw out forcibly"). Jesus told the disciples to teach new believers to do the same things He had taught them to do. Believers are operating underneath the same commission that Jesus gave to the disciples. It is only exceptionally that deliverance is permitted without the cooperation of the individual (Acts 16:18). The implication of Matthew 12:43-45 is that unless the doors are closed to the enemy through faith in Jesus, the latter state of the person could be even worse if more demons subsequently reoccupy the territory.

Enoch Wan, in "Spiritual Warfare and Victorious Christian," reminds the church,

> Overcoming demonization is not the monopoly of a few specialists or exorcists. All Christians could and should be victorious if following scriptural truth. (a). The position of Christians in Christ. Salvation is for the total person (body, soul, and/or Spirit) and is complete past, present, and future). (b). The provision for Christians in Christ. The victory over spirits is won by the power of prayer (Mark 9:29), the Word of God (Eph. 6:17-18), the blood of Christ (Rev. 12:11), and power of Jesus' name (Mark 9:39, Luke 9:49). (c). The promise for Christians' victory. Not only Christ's disciples were given authority to cast out demons (Mark 16:15-18, James 4:9). We are to regularly prepare for victory with positive attitude of being calm (1 Cor. 14:33), confident (1 John 4:4), and cautious (Eph. 6:10ff, 1 Pet. 5:8-9).[86]

Those who do the ministry of deliverance need to truly know who they are in Christ. They are in a process of exercising God-given authority over a spiritual being that, in terms of authority, is beneath us and whose source of power (Satan) is ultimately under the feet of Jesus. To exercise authority, one needs to be in a position of authority.

There are critics of deliverance who naively suggests that inner healing alone is needed. On the contrary, some practitioners of deliverance disparage the process of inner healing, saying that it is unnecessary. In practice, both are essential if full healing is to take place. "Unhealed and buried emotions are like food for the demonic, and if there is stored anger and emotional pain, release of this anger and pain will be necessary alongside the deliverance."[87] When the demons are spoken to and ordered to leave, they can manifest in the person without actually coming out. The way they manifest often provides clues to their nature. If, for example, there has been generational witchcraft, the body of the person can involuntarily take on a position indicative of a particular ritual. Another person might develop a sudden pain in a particular part of the body, and this can indicate a generational sickness of demonic origin that is being forced to manifest itself prior to being delivered. In practicing

---

[86] Enoch Wan, "Spiritual Warfare and Victorious Christian," http://www.enochwan.com/english/articles/pdf/Spiritual%20Warfare%20&%20Victorious%20Christian. pdf (Accessed November 27, 2017).

[87] Peter Horrobin, Healing through Deliverance: The Practice of Deliverance Ministry, vol. 2, (Grand Rapids: Chosen Books, 1991), 245.

deliverance ministry, demons are reminded of being under the authority of the Lord Jesus Christ and are ordered to speak the truth that Jesus Christ Himself would confirm as truth. This puts the demon in the same situation as the demon that controlled the Gadarene (Gerasene) demoniac. This demon was obliged to answer Jesus' questions and speak the truth. It may not be recommended to talk to demons as a normal means of deliverance yet may become a necessary part of the healing through deliverance. It is important to experience deliverance in life.

When deliverance is taking place, the person being delivered is generally aware of something happening at the spiritual level even if there are not any obvious manifestations. It is important to re-assure the individual when there are manifestations. The person can feel defiled or embarrassed by the demons, especially if they come out with vomiting or some other painfully obvious exit route. It is the spirits that are evil and unclean – not the person. Peter Horrobin points out some possible manifestations:

> cold, trembling, shaking, falling to the ground, palpitations, lumps in the throat, deep breathing, stirring in the stomach, screaming, pupils dilating, extending tongues, demonic tongues, sudden violent actions, running away, hissing, burping, swearing, snarling and barking, roaring, bellowing, slithering across like a snake. When any of the above manifestations occur, the Spirit-anointed servant of God has to exercise the authority in Jesus Christ and order the demon to leave without hurting either the individual or anyone else. There may be resistance, but if all the rights the demons had have been undercut, there should be no reason why they won't leave.[88]

Deliverance is but one aspect of our great salvation, so we need to ask the Lord to send His Angels to minister to the person for whom you are praying. It is very important to encourage and re-assure the person who is delivered from demons. Ask God to send the Holy Spirit to come and fill every area that has been vacated by the spirits.

---

[88] Horrobin, 247-249.

Anointing Equips to Overcome Strongholds with the Armor of God (Eph. 6:10-18)

Constant use of the armor of God provides that by which we may overcome demonic power in life and witness. Apostle Paul illustrates this from his own context.

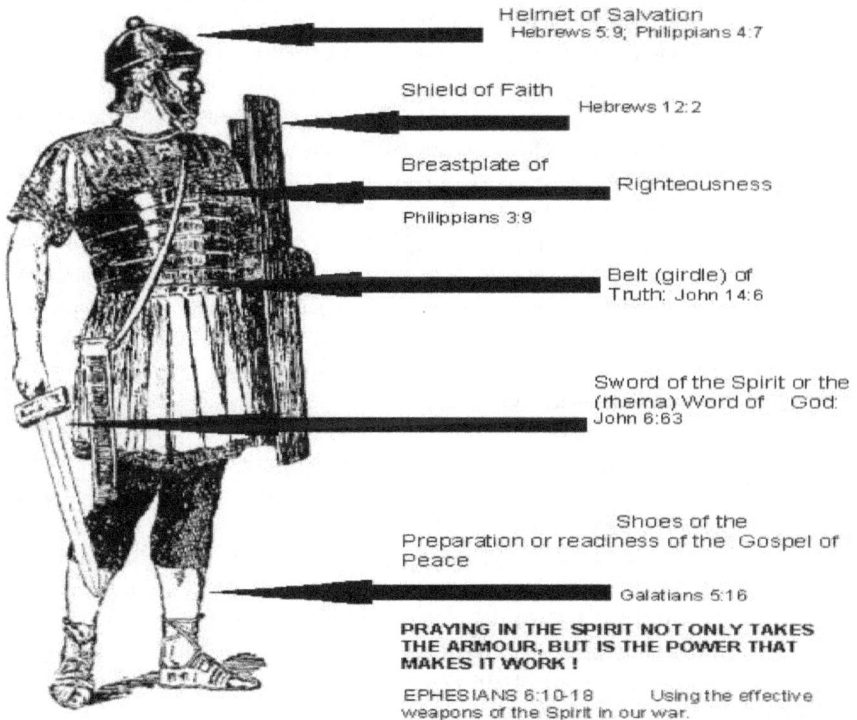

Taking the Whole Armour of God

Helmet of Salvation
Hebrews 5:9; Philippians 4:7

Shield of Faith
Hebrews 12:2

Breastplate of Righteousness
Philippians 3:9

Belt (girdle) of Truth: John 14:6

Sword of the Spirit or the (rhema) Word of God: John 6:63

Shoes of the Preparation or readiness of the Gospel of Peace
Galatians 5:16

PRAYING IN THE SPIRIT NOT ONLY TAKES THE ARMOUR, BUT IS THE POWER THAT MAKES IT WORK !

EPHESIANS 6:10-18   Using the effective weapons of the Spirit in our war.

Figure 3: The Armor of God for Spiritual Warfare, to Overcome Strongholds[89]

- Truth: It's like a girdle, it holds everything together and gives proper orientation to life. This is the truth of God, not the wisdom of men, and it needs to be the basis for how we look at everything: finances and friendships, activities and attitudes, family and fun, science and psychology. The total life must be governed by the truth of God as revealed in the scriptures.
- Righteousness: The breastplate is to guard the vital organs of life. Righteousness is imputed and imparted to us while we are in Christ. Both are meant for a genuine Christian life, rejecting ungodliness and worldly pleasures.

---

[89] James Dale Coldiron, "Spiritual Warfare Basics," (2004) http://www.voiceofthewatchman.org/audio/Spiritual%20Warfare%20Basics.htm (Accessed November 2017).

- Gospel of peace: Our feet are prepared to do the will of God because we have experienced the peace of God which the Gospel brings. A Christian witness advances in the context of all adversaries. How beautiful are the feet of those who bring good news (Rom. 10:15b)! Where the Gospel of peace is shared, relationship with God is restored and walls of hostility are broken down in a community.
- Faith: The large shield that gives overall protection. This is not ordinary faith but overcoming faith against satanic devices and schemes.
- Helmet of salvation: The joy and the assurance of salvation enable us to stand firm against all powers in the present and future.
- The sword of the Spirit: The Word of God. This is not merely the written Word but the spoken Word. Jesus Christ was privileged to use it against Satan in all three temptations recorded in the Gospels (Matt. 4:1-11, Luke 4:1-13). We overcome our opponent by the Word of Testimony (Rev. 12:11).
- Prayer. It brings wisdom and power to witnesses of the Gospel and ministers of the Word. "If any of you lacks wisdom, let him ask of God, Who gives to all liberally and without reproach, and it will be given to him" (Jas. 1:5). Prayer has the power to open our eyes to behold wondrous things out of God's Word (Ps. 119:18). Prayer will do more than a theological education to make the Bible an open book. Only people of prayer can understand the Bible.[90] Jesus prayed during His baptism, before His transfiguration, before His crucifixion, and before choosing the disciples. If the Son of God Himself found it significant to pray before or during the momentous events of His life, how much more we need to be engaged in prayer. Jesus taught His disciples how to pray while He was on earth (Luke 11:2-4). The key lessons of prayer are illustrated well by the apostles. It is praying with one accord (Acts 1:14); in faith (Jas. 5:15); humility (Luke 18:14); and in earnestness (Acts 12:5). Expressions like wrestling (Col. 4:12), constant (Rom. 1:9), and persistent in prayer (Luke 18:1-8) refer to how the church in the First Century made it as an opportunity to trust God in everything. Those who pray in other tongues make use of the gift for their own edification (1 Cor. 14:14-17). Prayer in the Spirit is an exercise done in the spiritual realm, rising above the ordinary sphere of life.

Summary

Holy Spirit is affirmed as a Person in the Godhead Who functions relationally. The Spirit-event on the day of Pentecost was the dynamic of Christian witness. The Spirit-anointing becomes a necessity for all because it is a distinct authorizing experience. It enlightens us to know the truth, enriches us to have Christ-likeness, empowers us to become passionate witnesses, and equips us to overcome strongholds in life and ministry. Anointing in the Spirit comes upon an individual by God, which enables one to carry out mission with faithfulness and integrity. The spiritual anointing sets apart a person's heart and mind with love, truth, and missional call of God to ministry.

---

[90] R A Torrey, *Power-Filled Living: How to Receive God's Best for Your Life,* (New Kensington, PA: Whitaker House, 1999), 60-63.

Holistic Christian mission is to be done in a relational paradigm. The Great Commission and the Great Commandment in the New Testament are the motivational pattern for us to engage in Christian witness. We proclaim the Gospel of grace, practice Christian discipleship, and demonstrate the power of God's Kingdom in deliverance. It is not restricted to any privileged one, rather, all who encounter Christ and become His disciples with Spirit-anointing are called to participate in the holistic mission.

CHAPTER 3
FOUNDATION AND FOCUS OF SPIRIT-ANOINTED WITNESS

Introduction

Christianity is not merely a set of beliefs, a creed to live by, or a sacramental fellowship, rather it is a reconciled relationship. God is a relational Being, existing in three Persons Who are distinct enough to relate to one another. Christ is the image of God (Phil 2:5-6). We look at Him, and we see God revealed in Him perfectly. Christ-event is the broad conception of Christianity itself. It is fundamentally an act of God in and through the Person and work of Christ ranging from incarnation to the imminent return of Christ. The questions, "What is the destiny of humanity?" Or "Where are we going?" stand at the center of all religions. Ideologies and philosophies in the World picture an ideal state, a utopia. But the Bible reveals faith that expresses hope in terms of the Kingdom of God. It is grounded in the assurance that there is One eternal living God Who has revealed Himself to people, with a purpose to accomplish through the chosen race.

Foundation of Spirit-Anointed Witness: Christ-Event

Christian mission is based not only on Trinity but very specifically on Christology. The mission of the Son is continued in the mission of the Spirit and made concrete by the mission of disciples in the World. David Bosch writes, "Christology, Pneumatology, and Missiology are thus brought into the closest relationship."[91] The Bible unfolds accounts of God's eternal plan and purpose of humanity in reconciling and redeeming from the power of sin and Satan, and to establish His reign over all creation. God chose to act through Christ to restore man to the intended relationship. It is through the revelation in Jesus Christ we come to know God. Christian mission is qualitatively unique because of Who Christ is and what He did for humanity.

Christ-event is the cornerstone of Christian theology. "Luke's pneumatology develops the Spirit-Christocentric functions in making the Spirit the chief witness to the Christ-event."[92] It signifies Jesus

---

[91] Bosch, Witness to the World, 241.
[92] Max Turner, *The Holy Spirit and Spiritual Gifts*, (Peabody, MA: Hendrickson Publishers, 1996), 40.

the Son of God effected eschatological salvation for humanity through His incarnation, death and resurrection, and Who is now the exalted Lord and coming King. "The salvation originated in God was effected historically by the death and resurrection of Christ and is appropriated experientially by God's people through the work of the Holy Spirit Who is also the key to Christian life 'between the times,' until the final consummation at Christ's *parousia.*"[93] The greatest miracle the World has ever seen is the incarnation of Jesus, the Son of God. The greatest manifestation of God's love is seen on the cross, and by the sacrifice of atonement we are redeemed and justified (Rom. 3:24-25). "God's grace is manifest in Christ, where grace and justice meet, opening the way for His kingdom to be established through forgiveness, reconciliation, and transformation in the power of the Holy Spirit."[94]

The resurrection of Jesus Christ is the greatest manifestation of God's power. It was a declaration and attestation that He is the Son of God and Lord (Rom. 1:4). Jesus' death on the cross would have remained meaningless without the resurrection. Arthur F Glasser writes "indeed had the resurrection not taken place there would have been no Christian Church and no worldwide missionary movement."[95] The early church witnessed to the resurrection of Jesus Christ (Acts 2: 32, 3:15). Christian Gospel is the message of victory over sin, Satan, and death.

The exaltation of Christ to the right hand of the Father signifies the honor, power, and glory He received in obedience to the will of the Father, fulfilling the Mission of salvation for humanity. Jesus continues the high priestly Mission for the Church on earth. The exalted Christ baptizes in the Holy Spirit. The One Who descended also ascended to fill the whole universe with gifts in the form of Apostles, Prophets, Evangelists, Pastors and Teachers for equipping the saints for the work of ministry (Eph. 4:10-12).

The imminent return of Jesus is to be foundational in Christian life. Robert E Coleman, in his article "The Hope of a Coming World Revival," writes, "...anticipation of our Lord's return is a summons to action."[96] We live in expectancy as we approach the latter days of the outpouring of the Holy Spirit and the coming of the Lord for effective witness. Veli-Matti Karkkainen writes, "The early Pentecostals relied upon the transforming, equipping power of the Holy Spirit, and their sense of eschatological expectation was such as to urge every believer to give testimony and render service before the Lord's return."[97]

Christ-event is the foundation in which incarnation, death, resurrection, exaltation, and imminent return of Christ are significant constructs for an anointed witness.

The Foundation: Christ-Event

The foundation of Sprit-anointed witness in holistic Christian mission is the Christ-event: incarnation, death, resurrection, exaltation, and the second coming of Christ. At the heart of the

---

[93] Gordon D Fee, God's Empowering Presence: The Holy Spirit in the Letters of Paul, (Peabody, MA: Hendrickson Publishers, 1994), 13.
[94] Craig Ott, Stephen J Strauss, Timothy C Tennent (eds), *Encountering Theology of Mission,* (Grand Rapids: Baker Academic, 2010), 87.
[95] Arthur F Glasser and Donald A McGavran (eds), *Contemporary Theology of Mission,* (Grand Rapids: Baker Books, 1983), 40.
[96] Robert E Coleman, "The Hope of a Coming World Revival," in Winter and Hawthorne (eds), 202.
[97] Veli-Matti Karkkainen, *Toward a Pneumatological Theology,* (Maryland, USA: University Press of America, 2002), 226.

Christian faith lies not so much a set of abstract ideas or beliefs but a person. We always insist that there is something special, something qualitatively different, about Jesus which sets Him apart from religious teachers or thinkers and demands careful consideration. In Jesus, the message and the messenger are one and the same. "The central challenge posed to the reader of the New Testament, especially the four Gospels, concerns the identity and relevance of Jesus Christ."[98] As Jesus was walking with the disciples in the region of Caesarea Philippi, He suddenly asked them a question, "Who do men say that I am?" The disciples replied with a variety of answers. Jesus asked His disciples the crucial question, "Who do you say that I am?" Peter replied, "You are the Christ, the Son of the living God" (Matt. 16:13-16). Here, we find that it was revealed by God the Father, as Jesus said. Our foundation is not based on vain speculation or logical inferences but by the revelatory act of God.

The purpose of writing the Gospels was to convey to people the good news of what God had planned and accomplished for their salvation. Everything in Christian Mission flows out of the work God has done in Jesus Christ. We are invited to participate in and give witness to that message, and Jesus is both message and the messenger. It is His life, His words, His deeds, and His promised return that embodies the salvation assured for us. David Bosch emphasizes that in the Old Testament there is no Christian Mission. "The decisive difference between Old and the New Testament is mission. The New Testament is essentially a book about mission."[99]

There are always two approaches to Christology. One can begin from one's doctrine of God and argue from that to Jesus, adopting a deductive, or what may be described as a downward approach. At the same time, one can start from the Jesus of the Gospels and see whether He leads us to God, following an inductive or upward approach. Both approaches largely go hand in hand in the New Testament. Norman Anderson writes, "the first disciples began with Jesus, the Man they knew so well as Teacher and had come to accept as Messiah. It seems to me that this is the natural starting point for us too."[100]

The Incarnation of Jesus Christ

It is generally taken for granted in a basic definition of Christianity that to confess Jesus as the Son of God is to confess His deity. It always has meant that Jesus is the pre-existent, second Person of the Trinity, Who for us men and our salvation became incarnate.[101] The incarnation of the eternal Word of God is indeed the greatest and most profound mystery which leads to the unique confession of the Christian Church: God, without ever ceasing to be God, actually became what He created in order to reconcile us to Himself. God's love is so great, His mercy and grace so persistent, and His desire to have us as His own so unrestrained that He performed an act of unparalleled condescension. The incredibly wonderful mystery the church confesses when we say Jesus Christ is both fully God and fully man is that God has joined Himself to us forever. As the eternal Son of God, the incarnate Jesus is fully God without reserve and fully man without reserve, and He is fully God and Man in His One Person. In the words of the Chalcedonian definition, "Jesus is fully God and fully man, one person

---

[98] Alister McGrath, *Understanding Jesus: Who Jesus Christ Is and Why He Matters,* (Grand Rapids,MI: Academic Books,1987), 17.
[99] Bosch, in Sunquist, 199.
[100] Norman Anderson, *The Mystery of the Incarnation,* (Downers Grove: InterVarsity Press, 1979), 12.
[101] James D G Dunn, Christology in the Making: A New Testament Inquiry into the Origins of the Doctrine of the Incarnation, (Grand Rapids: Eerdmans Publishing, 1989), 13.

existing in two natures now and forevermore"[102] In other words, the incarnate Son of God is exactly as God is and exactly as we are. By becoming human, the eternal Son of the eternal Father took our humanity into union with Himself in order to bridge the divide between God and man; thus, God and man are united in the incarnate One. Jesus is not a split personality with His divine and human natures in conflict. In scripture Jesus never spoke of either His deity or His humanity as separate from Himself; He always spoke and acted as one person. There were several Christological controversies which arose in early centuries concerning the person of Jesus Christ: Docetism, which taught that Jesus only seemed to be a man, His body was only an apparition. "He couldn't have exposed Himself to the experiences of human life. The humanity of Jesus, His physical nature, was simply an illusion, not a reality, Jesus was more like a ghost, an apparition, than a human being."[103] This theory denied the validity of the incarnation. The Apostle John refuted this view in 1 John 4:2-3, 1:1-3.

Another early heresy, Ebionism denied the virgin birth of Jesus, maintained that Jesus was born to Joseph and Mary in the normal fashion.[104] And taught that the eternal Christ was united with the human Jesus when John baptized Jesus; some of them believed that "the Christ" left Jesus on the cross, pointing to His cry, "My God, My God, why have You forsaken Me?" (Matt. 27:46). According to this view, Jesus died just as a man not as God-Man. Many believe that 1 John 5:6-8 is a refutation of this heresy.

Monarchianism was another heresy in the early centuries. In order to oppose Trinitarianism, in an effort to preserve absolute monotheism, they presented one of two points of view. The Adoptionist or Dynamic Monarchians maintained that Jesus was God only in the sense that a power or influence from the Father rested upon His human person.[105] The Modalist Monarchians, also called Sabellians (from Sabellius – Third Century), taught that in the Godhead the only differentiation was a mere succession of modes or operations. However, this is refuted by the separate presence of the three Persons of the triune Godhead at Jesus' baptism by John the Baptist (Matt. 3:16-17, Luke 3:21-22). Arianism denied the eternality and full deity of the Word Who became incarnate as Jesus Christ. The "logos" was not eternal but was created by God at some finite point. The slogan of Arianism became, "there was a time when He was not."[106] This heresy is promoted in our day by both Jehovah's Witnesses and Mormons (The Church of Jesus Christ of Latter Day Saints). Charles Taze Russel, founder of the Watchtower Bible and Tract Society, which later became known as the Jehovah's Witnesses, described Jesus Christ as the highest of all Jehovah's creation, so also, He was the first, the direct creation of God, the only begotten, and then, He, as Jehovah's power, and in His name, created all things – angels, principalities, and powers, as well as the earthly creation. The Mormon author James E Talmadge affirmed the preexistence of Christ before His conception by Mary and birth in Bethlehem, but he taught that Jesus was not God, a member of the Trinity. Talmadge also wrote, He had lived with the Father as an unembodied spirit, the first born of the Father's children.

---

[102] Stephen J Wellum, "The Deity of Christ in the Gospels," in Christopher W Morgan and Robert A Peterson (eds), *The Deity of Christ*, (Wheaton: Crossway, 2011), 62.
[103] J N D Kelly, *Early Christian Doctrines*, (New York: Harper and Row, 1960), 141.
[104] Millard J Erickson, *Christian Theology*, (Grand Rapids: Baker House, 1986), 694, (From Justin Martyr, *Dialogue with Trypho*, 47).
[105] Erickson, 733.
[106] Erickson, 696.

Eutychianism was another heresy developed against Nestorianism. It held that in the incarnate Christ, deity and humanity were blended into one nature.[107] As a result, Jesus was not fully divine, and yet He was more than human; He had a *theanthropic* nature but was not the *theanthropic* person, the God-Man. Monothelitism was a variation of this view, Christ had two natures, but only one will. Even though Jesus could express His human will in the sense of wish or desire, as voiced in His prayer in the Garden of Gethsemane (Matt. 26:39, 42), His personal will in the sense of moral choice always followed the will of God the Father. The Church in early centuries worked hard at times to convene councils to refute all heresies. Formulations of Church councils succeeded up to a certain level to settle those issues which culminated at the council of Chalcedon (AD 451). The accounts of the incarnate life of Jesus in the Gospels help us to draw accurate conclusions concerning the relationship between the divine and human natures in the person of Jesus Christ.

So, the starting point for all theological reflection is the incarnation. However, when we say that in the incarnation Jesus took on humanity, we are not talking about our sin-filled humanity. For the humanity of Jesus was not the humanity of sinful human beings, rather the humanity possessed by Adam and Eve from their creation and before their fall. His humanity was certainly more compatible with deity than is the humanity we now observe. The impeccability of Jesus is understood from the Gospels. He was sinless at conception and birth (Luke 1:34-35), was subject to temptation and falling into sin, and of itself His nature was as the sinless human natures of Adam and Eve until they disobeyed God and sinned. Nevertheless, because Jesus' nature was joined with His divine nature in one person, He not only did not sin when tempted by the Devil or at any time later in His earthly life, but He would not sin.

The incarnate Son reveals the knowledge of God: Humanity is left with broken and corrupted knowledge of God due to sin. John Webster notes, "sin involves forfeit knowledge of God and the replacement of that knowledge by illusion. We are fallen creatures, we do not know, and we do not know what we do not know."[108] The crucial thing is the divide He came to bridge between how we want to know God and how He actually wants to be known. The advent of God the Son revealed that the God of Israel, Who created the heavens and the earth, and Who brought all creatures into existence, the Sovereign over all the universe, is a complex unity. God is God the Father, God the Son, and God the Spirit, and is all the while one God. Jesus asserted, "no one knows the Son except the Father, and no one knows the Father except the Son and anyone to whom the Son chooses to reveal Him" (Matt 11:27). In other words, to know the Son is to know the Father: "If you had known Me, you would have known My Father also...Whoever has seen Me has seen the Father" (John 14:7, 9).

The incarnation shows the depths of divine love. God's love reaches everyone in the World for their salvation (John 3:16). How do we claim God is love in a World of war and crime? According to the Bible war is not caused by God; it is rather the result of sin in the World (Gen. 4:3-8, Matt. 15:19). Humanity is given freedom to choose right and wrong from creation itself. When they make a wrong choice, that creates conflicts and wars. When people have greed and selfishness in their hearts, they start a fight in order to get what is not theirs. God is always on the side of the right which is revealed in the Bible.

---

[107] Jaroslav Pelican, *The Christian Tradition*, (Chicago: University of Chicago, 1971), 262-63.
[108] John Webster, "Principles of Systematic Theology," *International Journal of Systematic Theology* 11, no.1 (January 2009), 61-62.

The Lord is a warrior" (Ex. 15:3) is not to be interpreted out of context but, the context is the destruction of Egyptian army who enslaved Israelites. We find a prophetical announcement, there will be a time when it is required to fight (Joel 3:9-10). There is no contradiction for God to be both the Lord Who battles unrighteousness and also loves peace.[109]

John writes, "this is how God showed His love among us, He sent His one and only Son into the world that we might live through Him. This is love: not that we loved God, but that He loved us and sent His Son as atonement for our sins (1 John 4:9-10). If we want to know what Biblical forgiveness looks like, we go back to the story of how Joseph forgave his brothers who sold him into slavery (Gen. 50:15-21). If we want to know what repentance is, we think of the story Jesus told of the return of the prodigal to his father (Luke 15:11-32). And if we want to know what divine love is in our sort of World and the evidence for it, we tell the story of the incarnation and the atonement: Christmas and Easter.[110]

The incarnation results in granting eternal life. The knowledge which Jesus speaks is not speculative, theoretical, or philosophical knowledge, rather the intimate fellowship He has eternally enjoyed in relation to the Father and the Spirit. To know God is to participate in the very life and love that the Father has for the Son by the power and presence of the Spirit (John 14:20). Jesus said, "This is eternal life, that they know You the only true God, and Jesus Christ Whom You have sent" (John 17:3). The biblical confession that "there is one God, and there is one mediator between God and men, the man Christ Jesus" (1 Tim. 2:5) is theologically coherent because only God knows God, and so only God can make Himself known.

Due to the fact that God entered the World in and as Jesus Christ, the meaning of God and the meaning of the World are given definitive expression in Him. Christ is both the Creator and the new creation. "Thus, our theology must be explicitly Christocentric, not as a matter of arbitrary theological method, but as a matter of necessity, for He is the Truth of God and the truth of the world in His one person."[111] It is the essence of Christian faith that the event of the incarnation is final, decisive, once for all. For this reason, it is not enough that the event be remembered in the tradition of the Church, the tradition cannot become a substitute for it.

When the church preaches the birth of Christ, it is not just because this is an event of historical significance which deserves to be commemorated, it is because this event is, literally, the beginning of the Gospel. For the Gospel consists in that relation to sinful men upon which Christ entered by being born as man; and the message of Christmas remains in the air unless the first two words of the angelic announcement become true: unto you is born this day in the city of David a savior, which is Christ the Lord (Luke 2:11) there must be an extension of the incarnation to include us among those to whom He is born, and with whom He entered into relation.[112]

---

[109] Matt Slick, "Is the Lord a God of Peace or War?" https://carm.org/lord-god-peace-or-war. (Accessed December 10, 2017).

[110] Graham Arthur Cole, *The God Who Became Human: A Biblical Theology of Incarnation,* (Downers Grove: InterVarsity Press, 2013), 160.

[111] John C Clark and Marcus Peter Johnson, The Incarnation of God: The Mystery of the Gospel as the Foundation of Evangelical Theology, (Wheaton: Crossway, 2015), 234.

[112] George S Hendry, *The Gospel of the Incarnation,* (Philadelphia: Westminister Press, 1959), 162.

The Death of Jesus Christ

Christian faith and the message of a missionary is focused on the work God has done through Jesus Christ rather than on the works we do. Who is Jesus Christ? Our first attempt to answer this question connects with historical evidence. The historical evidence we possess concerning the origins of Christianity and the character of its early years is most easily explained on the basis of the existence of Jesus as a historical figure. Jesus was a first century Jew Who lived in Palestine in the reign of Tiberius Caesar and was executed by crucifixion under Pontius Pilate. The Roman historian Tacitus refers to Christians deriving their name from Christ, Who was executed at the hands of the Procurator Pontius Pilate in the reign of Tiberius (Annals, xv, 44, 3).

Luke gives clear expression to his certainty that in the cross God was working out His purpose of salvation. Peter told the men of Jerusalem that Jesus was delivered up by the determinate counsel and foreknowledge of God (Acts 2:23). This means more than that God knew beforehand what would happen. He planned that the Messiah should be given over to death. Calvary is not to be regarded as a tragedy or a martyrdom. The prayer meeting in Acts 4 reiterates the truth. All concerned, Herod, Pilate, Gentiles, and Israelites alike, the praying group affirmed, "were gathered together to do whatsoever Your hand and Your counsel foreordained to come to pass" (Acts 4:27ff). The cross must be seen as the accomplishment of the divine purpose. This thought is found in many passages in Acts (1:6, 3:18, 8:35, 26:22ff). "Now, if Christ's death is in fulfilment of prophecies made Centuries beforehand, then clearly the primary thing is the will of Him Who caused those prophecies to be made. The events which culminated in the crucifixion on the hill called Calvary cannot be said to have taken place by chance."[113]

Crucifixion was one of the most painful methods of execution invented by man. Those who endured it had to undergo excruciating agonies. In the Lucan perspective, the suffering was not altogether an unmixed evil. Suffering was the pathway the Christ must tread to bring to the World its greatest good. It has been proved true that Christians' greatest contribution to the service of God and their fellows has been along the path of suffering.

"Paul the Apostle takes Jesus' existence as a fact which does not require demonstration and concentrates upon establishing and defending the significance of His life, death, and resurrection."[114] The subject of his preaching was Christ crucified (1 Cor. 1:23). The power lying behind the Gospel proclamation is the cross of Jesus Christ (v. 18). The cross is the place where God and man meet. It is recognized as the demonstration of God's love upon us where we receive the offer of God's grace. Paul links Jesus' death and resurrection together as the two elements of his Gospel. Jesus was put to death for our trespasses and raised for our justification (Rom. 4:24-25). He also makes a clear distinction between the event of the death of Christ and the significance of this event. That Christ died is a simple matter of history; that Christ died for our sins is the Gospel itself. "The Christian faith is based upon certain historical events but, is not to be identified with these events alone; rather, it is to be identified with an interpretation of these events."[115] It is significant to know the truth and relevance of the event. For Paul, Jesus was the bearer of Salvation to sinful man. The benefits from the Christ-event are the forgiveness of sins, reconciliation to God, and the hope of resurrection.

[113] Leon Morris, *The Cross in the New Testament*, (Grand Rapids: Eerdmans Publishing, 1972), 123.
[114] McGrath, 19.
[115] McGrath, 23.

Atonement

The term "atonement" refers to a reconciled state of at-one-ness between parties that were formerly alienated in some manner. Numerous theories of atonement developed in the past enable us to understand God's act of salvation accomplished on the cross through His Son. The reason human beings need to be reconciled to God is because of their sin and guilt. Sin is an objective reality that separates sinners from a Holy God. Thomas R Schreiner defines the Penal Substitution View as follows:

The Father, because of His love for human beings, sent His Son (Who offered Himself willingly and gladly) to satisfy God's justice, so that Christ took the place of sinners. The punishment and penalty we deserved was laid on Jesus Christ instead of us, so that in the cross both God's holiness and love are manifested.[116]

The claim here is that this is the heart and soul of an evangelical view of the atonement and it functions as the anchor and foundation of all other dimensions of the atonement. Reconciliation between God and humans doesn't become a reality merely on the basis of repentance and a desire for forgiveness. Reconciliation is a precious reality, and it is anchored in the sin-bearing work of Christ on the cross by which the wrath of God was appeased. The penalty for sin is death (Rom. 6:23). Sinners deserve eternal punishment in Hell from God Himself because of their sin and guilt. God's Holy anger is directed (Rom. 1:18) against all who have sinned and fall short of the glory of God (Rom. 3:23). Based on God's love, He sent Jesus Christ to bear the punishment of our sins. Christ died in our place, took to Himself our sin (2 Cor. 5:21) and guilt (Gal. 3:10), and bore our penalty so that we might receive forgiveness of sins. We love God because He loved us first (1 John 4:19). Such forgiveness wouldn't be ours apart from the death and resurrection of Jesus Christ. Death and resurrection are well integrated in the atonement. The doctrine of the penal substitution theory states that "God gave Himself in the Person of His Son to suffer instead of us, the death, punishment, and curse due to fallen humanity as the penalty for sin."[117]

Sinfulness of humanity on one side, and the holiness of God on the other side, require a sacrifice. There must be a penal substitute. When we think of Old Testament sacrifices, the lying of hand on animals most likely means that the animal functions as a substitute for a person. The sin of human beings is transferred, so to speak, to the animal. Ultimately the blood of animals cannot atone for human sin (Heb. 10:4). Romans 3:21-26 is a key text on penal substitution. God set forth Christ as a propitiatory sacrifice by virtue of Jesus' death. The terms *hilasterion* and *haima* point back to the Old Testament *cultus* and sacrificial system. The term *hilasterion* includes the sense of the averting of God's wrath – the appeasement or satisfaction of His righteousness. To be more precise, the term includes both notions, expiation and propitiation. The argument in Romans 1:18-30 provokes the question, how can God's wrath be averted. We find in Romans 3:25-26 that God's wrath has been satisfied or appeased in the death of Christ. Millard J Erickson provides rightly the implications of substitutionary atonement,

---

[116] Thomas R Schreiner, "Penal Substitution View," in James Beilby and Paul R Eddy (eds), *The Nature of the Atonement: Four Views*, (Downers Grove: IVP Academic, 2006), 67.
[117] Steve Jeffrey, Michael Ovey, and Andrew Sach, *Pierced for Our Transgressions: Rediscovering the Glory of Penal Substitution*, (Nottingham, PA: IVP, 2017), 1.

the substitutionary theory of the atoning death of Christ, when grasped in all complexity, is a rich and meaningful truth. The penal-substitution theory confirms the biblical teaching of the total depravity of all human beings. He is righteous and so loving that sacrifice for sin had to be provided. There is no salvation but by grace, and specifically the death of Christ. There is security for the believer in his or her relationship to God, for the basis of the relationship, Christ's sacrificial death, is complete and permanent. We must never take lightly the salvation which we have. We must always be grateful for what He has done; we must love Him in return and emulate His giving character.[118]

Christ's death is interpreted in a wide variety of ways. Each of the theories possesses a dimension of the truth. Christ is the substitute, an example before us, demonstrated the great extent of God's love, triumphed over the forces of sin and death, and rendered satisfaction to the Father for our sin. Though there are attempts to harmonize theories of atonement, Penal Substitution Atonement (PSA) is the essential to correctly understanding and articulating the work of Christ.[119] Penal substitution is not all that needs to be said about the atonement precisely because of its God-centered focus. God sent His Son because of His great love for sinners (John 3:16, Rom. 5:6-10, 8:32, 1 John 4:10). The Son gladly gave His life for sinners. It was His delight to do the will of God (Heb. 10:5-10), and He surrendered His life voluntarily (John 10:18).

The Resurrection of Jesus Christ

All branches of systematic theology have tended to underestimate the significance of the resurrection of Christ. We notice the apologetic significance of the resurrection as an attestation of the deity of Christ and the value of His substitutionary death. The resurrection of Christ is normally held to be a proof of the future resurrection of the saints. Norman Geisler writes, "of all the wonderful things Jesus taught them about love (Matt. 22:36-37), non-retaliation (Matt. 5), and the Kingdom of God (Matt. 13), the prevailing of Apostolic preaching was none of these; it was the resurrection of Christ."[120]

It is noteworthy that the meaning of the official name of Christ, namely, Lord Jesus Christ, is substantiated by His resurrection. The title Lord, usually regarded as a declaration of His deity and authority over all creation, is based on the assumption that Jesus Christ is the Son of God.[121] The supreme proof of His deity is the solid fact of His resurrection. This was the subject of Peter's preaching at Pentecost (Acts 2:22ff) and his next sermon in the temple (3:12-26). It was also the content of the message before the Sanhedrin (4:8ff). Peter presented the Gospel at the household of Cornelius with the same theme (Acts 10:40). The apostles went everywhere with great power and continued to testify to the resurrection of the Lord Jesus Christ.

It is significant to note that "to be a witness of the resurrection" was also a pre-requisite to be chosen as an apostle" (Acts 1:21-22, 1 Cor. 9:1). In the title "Christ" as attributed to the Lord Jesus is embodied the hope of Israel for a Messiah to deliver them from their sins. If Christ had not been raised from the dead, it is evident that His claim to Messiahship would have been thus destroyed. Conversely,

[118] Erickson, 822.
[119] Patrick Alexander Early, Articulating the Doctrine of Penal Substitution Atonement in the 21st Century: Integrating Relational Paradigm with the Metaphor of Kaleidoscope, (unpublished dissertation, Western Seminary, Portland, April 2017).
[120] Norman Geisler, *Systematic Theology, vol 2*, (Minneapolis: Bethany House, 2003), 623.
[121] John F Walvoord, *Jesus Christ Our Lord,* (Chicago: Moody Press, 1969), 207.

the fact of His resurrection establishes His right to be Israel's Messiah in the past as well as in the future. "Jesus," the third title attributed to Christ, meaning YHWH saves, was His human name bestowed by the angel. He was given this name because He would save His people from their sins (Matt. 1:21). His work as Savior, however, while inevitably related to His death on the cross, also demanded His resurrection. According to John 12:27, where Christ prayed in regard to His death, "Father save Me from this hour," He didn't anticipate merely deliverance from death but prayed that if it were necessary to die, He would experience complete deliverance from death in His resurrection. It is the uniform presentation of scripture that His resurrection is a necessary counterpart to His work in death, and apart from His resurrection, His death would have become meaningless (John 11: 25, Rom. 5:10, 8:34, 10:9, Heb. 5:7). The Resurrection of Christ is, therefore, the proof of His person and of that which His person effected, namely, His work on the cross.

The empty tomb and the resurrection appearances were the strongest evidences for the genuineness of Jesus' resurrection. The story spread by the bribed guards that His disciples stole Jesus' body while they slept had been widely circulated by the Jews (Matt. 28: 15). "This story was obviously false. If the disciples had stolen the body, why were they willing to suffer persecution and death for their proclamation of Jesus resurrection?"[122] Luke declared that Jesus showed Himself to the apostles and gave many convincing proofs that He was alive. He appeared to them over a period of forty days (Acts 1:3). Out of ten appearances, five of them were on the day of resurrection and the rest in the forty days of resurrection ministry. Christ's resurrection as the great proof or sign of both His Sonship and Messiahship is the theme of the Gospels. When the un- believing Jews asked Jesus for a sign or proof of His authority to cleanse the temple, He pointed to His future resurrection, "destroy this temple, and in three days I will raise it up" (John 2:19). "The resurrection of Jesus is the great and invincible proof of Who He is and what He has accomplished on behalf of His people."[123]

The Exaltation of Jesus Christ

The resurrection of Christ has not only a backward look toward the cross demonstrating the power of God in salvation, it is also the doorway to His present work in heaven. Orr states, "The resurrection of Jesus is everywhere viewed as the commencement of His exaltation. Resurrection, Ascension, Exaltation to the throne in universal dominion go together as parts of the same transaction."[124] Several important aspects of His ministry were contingent upon the fact of His resurrection: sending of the Holy Spirit (John 14:26, 15:26, 16:7), bestowing eternal life (John 11:25, 12:24-25), head of the Church and the new creation (Eph. 1:20-23, 1 Cor. 15:45b, 1 Pet. 2:4-5, 9), intercession at the right hand of the Father (Heb. 7:25, 1 John 2:1), bestowal of gifts to the Church as apostles, prophets, evangelists, pastors and teachers (Eph. 4:11-13). Impartation of spiritual power (Matt. 28:18, Eph. 1:17-23, Acts 1:8), raising of believers to a new position in Christ (Eph. 2:5-6), raised from the dead as first-fruit in anticipation of the future resurrection of all the believers (1 Cor. 15:20-23, Phil. 3:20-21).

---

[122] Charles R Swindoll and Roy B Zuck (eds), *Understanding Christian Theology*, (Nashville: Thomas Nelson Publishers, 2003), 356.
[123] Paul Washer, *The Gospel's Power and Message*, (Grand Rapids: Reformation Heritage Books, 2012), 208-209.
[124] James Orr, *The Resurrection of Jesus*, (Eugene, OR: Wipf and Stock Publishers, 1997), 21.

The Imminent Return of Jesus Christ

The second coming of Jesus Christ is part of the Christian *kerygma*. John tells us that in the upper room Jesus promised His disciples, "And if I go and prepare a place for you, I will come back and take you with Me, that you also may be where I am" (John 14:3). At Jesus ascension, the angels appeared and said to the disciples, "men of Galilee why do you stand here, looking at the sky? This same Jesus Who has been taken from you into heaven, will come back in the same way you have seen Him go into heaven" (Acts 1:11). The definiteness of the event was proclaimed by the apostles as appointed by God (Acts 3:19-21). Paul wrote on several occasions and assured the Church of the precious hope in Christ (Phil. 3:20-21, 1 Thess. 4:15-16). Other authors also clearly mentioned the second coming (Heb. 9:28, 1 Pet. 1:7, 13, 1 John 2:28). Christ's second coming will be personal in character and visible in nature. The imminence of the second coming of Christ is emphasized in the scripture. Jesus urged His disciples to be ready for the coming (Matt. 24-25). There is a repeated emphasis that we are to wait eagerly (Rom. 8:19-25, Titus 2:13, Jude 21).

Focus of the Spirit-anointed Witness: The Kingdom of God

The Kingdom of God (*bassileia tou theou* – Gk) was God's overall sovereign rule in Judaism and they believed that God would act to establish His Kingdom at the end of the age. George Eldon Ladd writes,

Our central thesis is that the Kingdom of God is the redemptive reign of God dynamically active to establish His rule among men, and that this Kingdom, which will appear as an apocalyptic act at the end of the age, has already entered into human history in the person and mission of Jesus to overcome evil, to deliver men from its power, and to bring them into the blessings of God's reign.[125]

The Kingdom of God is an eschatological term belonging primarily to the category of time rather than space. It refers to the end *(eschaton* – Gk). The expression, "the time is fulfilled," indicates that the Kingdom of God is ultimately tied to Jewish messianic expectations. It is evident in the covenant God made with Abraham that through his seed all the peoples on earth will be blessed (Gen. 12:3). The hope of the restoration of God's glory was yearned for by the prophets in history. It is reflected in such Psalms as 2 and 72 which were originally composed for the coronation of Davidic kings and in time came to be understood as pointing to the "great king" of the future. Though the people of Israel failed to keep covenant with God, YHWH, gave themselves to idolatry, sexual immorality, and injustice, there was a small remnant who were doing His will. They returned to the Lord and looked forward to the day of salvation. A group of writers emerged in Israel known as *apocalyptists*. They were longing for a crashing end to the present age, with its evil and oppression, and to usher in the age to come as an age of the Spirit – an age of righteousness and justice. John the Baptist announced the nearness of the future, "repent, for the Kingdom of God is near." There is a sense of urgency for the day of the Lord. The return of the prophetic voice, and the people were prepared to live with great anticipation. Some were baptized by the hands of John the Baptist as an outward expression of their

---

[125] Ladd, 91.

repentance. However, the Kingdom of God didn't appear with John the Baptist, instead, he was arrested and eventually murdered.

The kingdom of God is a central teaching point of Jesus Christ right up to the last hours of His earthly life. He appeared to the disciples after the resurrection with many proofs and spoke about the Kingdom of God (Acts 1:3-8). It was true that the disciples were hearing it three years before the death and resurrection of their master. As Jesus was about to ascend, they asked, "Lord, will you at this time restore the Kingdom to Israel?" It shows the Kingdom of God was central for Jesus and the focus of His disciples. References to Kingdom occur forty-five times in Luke and eight times in Acts.

Church and the Kingdom

None of the sayings in the Gospels equate the church with the Kingdom though there is obviously a close connection between the two. The declaration of Jesus, "I will build My Church, and the gates of hades will not overcome it" is linked with Jesus' saying to Peter, "I will give you the keys of the Kingdom of heaven" (Matt. 16:18-19). From this one might infer that the church is a synonym for the Kingdom. As George Ladd argues, this is pressing metaphorical language too far and he maintained that the kingdom is thought of as the reign of God.[126] Church is the concrete manifestation of God's sovereign rule in our hearts. Erickson writes,

The kingdom can be found wherever God rules in human hearts. But more than that, it is found wherever His will is done. Thus, the Kingdom was present in heaven even before the creation of humans, for the angels were subject to and obeyed God. They are included within His Kingdom now and will be in the future. But they never have been and never will be part of the Church. The church is the only manifestation of the Kingdom.[127]

The church is the instrument of the Kingdom. We see the emphasis of Luke's Gospel continued in Acts where the foundation and expansion of the church are found. Augustine identified the kingdom of God with the Church which continues in Catholic doctrine. The Church is the result of the coming of God's Kingdom into the World through the mission of Jesus Christ. It is the church's mission to witness the Kingdom, testifying to God's redeeming acts in Christ both past and future. This is illustrated by the commission Jesus gave to the twelve (Matt. 10:7), and to the seventy (Luke 10:9). The only specific instruction given in both instances is "as you go, preach this message, the kingdom of God is near." There are different expressions in relation with the Kingdom found in the Gospels, to seize the kingdom, to enter the Kingdom, to seek the kingdom, the mystery of the kingdom, the keys of the kingdom, the least/greatest in the kingdom. It is reinforced by the proclamation of the apostles in the book of Acts.

The Kingdom of God is God's Action and Gift

The fact is established from the very beginning. The angel Gabriel promises Mary, "and the Lord God will give Him the throne of His father David" (Luke 1:32). Jesus responds to those who claim He casts out demons through the power of Beelzebub, "but if I drive out demons by the finger of God, then the Kingdom of God has come to you" (Luke 11:20). At the last supper Jesus assures His apostles,

---

[126] Ladd, 112.
[127] Erickson, 1042.

"I confer on you a Kingdom, just as My Father conferred one on Me so that you may eat and drink at My table in My Kingdom and sit on thrones, judging the twelve tribes of Israel (Luke 22:29-30). It is the Father's good pleasure to give the disciples the Kingdom (Luke 12:32) and they are to pray that it comes (Luke 11:2). The exact time of its coming depends on the Father; Jesus explained it to the disciples, "it is not for you to know the times or dates the Father has set by His own authority" (Acts 1:7).

The Kingdom of God is at Hand

Jesus announced the time is fulfilled; the kingdom of God is at hand. This is the declaration of the great messianic prophesy of Isaiah 61:1-2a, about the coming of God's anointed One Who would proclaim good news to the poor and the coming of the year of the Lord's favor, had in fact been fulfilled in His own coming (Luke 4:6-30). God's great eschatological day had finally dawned through His own compassionate ministry, in healing the sick, casting out demons, and eating with sinners. "The Kingdom of God" means the destruction of Satan's reign and salvation for the Christians. The World is divided between darkness and light, between the power of God and the power of Satan (cf. Acts 26:18). Miracles demonstrate that the reign of Satan is being overcome. Therefore, Jesus, when He is accused of casting out demons by Beelzebub, says, "If Satan is divided himself, how can his kingdom stand. I say this because you claim that I drive out demons by Beelzebub. Now, if I drive out demons by the finger of God, then the Kingdom of God has come to you" (Luke 11:18-20, cf. 4:40-43). Luke joins the preaching of the Kingdom with power and authority over demons and to cure diseases (8:1-2, 9:1-2, 11, 10:9). Jesus' words about the cure of the woman with an infirmity explains well the meaning of the Kingdom, "Then, shouldn't this woman, a daughter of Abraham, whom Satan has kept bound for eighteen years be set free on the Sabbath day from what bound her?" (Luke 13:16). The Kingdom of God is associated with salvation. On the occasion when the rich young official refuses to give up his possessions and follow him, Jesus observes, "How hard it is for the rich to enter the Kingdom of God. Indeed, it is easier for the camel to go through the eye of a needle than for a rich man to enter the Kingdom of God" (Luke 18:24-25). To enter the Kingdom of God has to be equivalent to being saved. Luke again associates the Kingdom of God and salvation in Jesus' answer to Peter. Jesus assures him, "there is no one who has left house or wife or brothers or children, for the sake of the Kingdom of God, who will not receive manifold in this time and in the age to come eternal life" (Luke 18: 29-30). Eternal life is the enjoyment of salvation. Paul addressed the leaders of the Roman Jews in testifying to the Kingdom of God and tried to convince them about Jesus both from the law of Moses and from the prophets (Acts 28:23). But when they disagreed, he concluded using the words of Isaiah 6:10, "Make the heart of this people calloused, make their ears dull and close their eyes. Otherwise they might see with their eyes, hear with their ears, understand with their hearts, and turn and be healed."

The liberal theologians of the 19th century took a purely present Kingdom approach resulting in social liberalism. Albrecht Ritschl (1822-89), argued that the Kingdom of God was this World, monistic and ethical in character, a picture ultimately derived from Kantian ethical idealism.[128] The emphasis was very much on man's working out of these values within our World today; any reference

---

[128] Albrecht Ritschl, in Wendell Willis (ed), *The Kingdom of God in 20th Century Interpretation*, (Peabody, MA: Hendrickson Publishers, 1987), 2.

to the future was eliminated. However, this assumption was challenged later by a revolution in New Testament studies at the turn of the 20th Century. Johannes Weiss, Albert Schweitzer, and others rediscovered the eschatological element of Jesus' teaching on the Kingdom of God. Their view, later known as the consistent eschatology, discounts the concept of an already present kingdom in Jesus' teaching, claiming that He points only to an entire future, apocalyptic reality, which is to arrive by a cataclysmic in-breaking of Jesus into time.[129] It pointed to the New Testament message of the Kingdom of God as one that will be established by God Himself. The future was God's prerogative, not man's doing, even the natural sequence of historic events that led ultimately to this Kingdom. C H Dodd, the father of realized eschatology, represents an opposing view to that of Weiss and Schweitzer, arguing that the apocalyptic elements in Jesus' teaching are to be taken as merely symbolic, for the Kingdom of God is already a present fact with no future fulfilment. "The eschaton has moved from the future to the present, from the sphere of eschaton into that of realized experience."[130] George Elden Ladd must be credited for bringing back to the evangelical agenda the topic of the Kingdom of God. Ken Gnanakan made a significant effort: "We are challenged to reconcile the two, creatively, underlining both the immanence of the Kingdom in its impact on life today as well as the mystery of the Kingdom as something to be fully revealed in the future. Jesus' message was neither other-worldly, idealistic dream, nor a totally present reality. The two need to be interlinked. It is in the interdependence of the present and the future that the fullest meaning of the Kingdom will be seen."[131]

The Church Witnesses Kingdom

The Church is an eschatological community because it is a Christological reality. The central point in God's redemptive activity is the cross of Jesus Christ accompanied by His victorious resurrection. The Gospel of the Kingdom is inseparable from the Word of the cross, for it is the message of the cross that brings salvation. For Paul, it is the cross that represents both the power and wisdom of God. It is at the cross that we see Jesus as the High Priest. All three aspects of the three-fold anointed offices of Prophet, Priest, and King, are foundational for the kingdom of God as it finds its expression in the community of believers. The unique Christ-event of the cross and resurrection mark the beginning of the new age and the beginning of the end of the old age. The early Church expressed its faith in Christ the King and pledged its allegiance to Him in that short yet, powerful confession, Jesus is Lord. The Pentecostal-event was crucial for the launching and constitution of the Christian Church, the new eschatological community bound together by their loyalty to the risen Lord and the common experience of the Spirit. J D G Dunn writes, "Like the resurrection of Jesus, Pentecost was seen by early Christians as the precursor of the end and as the beginning of a whole new epoch of salvation history."[132]

In other words, the church and its mission today must be seen from the standpoint of the future to draw out the true significance of its being in God. The focus of the church should be the Kingdom of God in the future. Jesus Christ taught this fact in relation with His teaching on "the effort to enter

---

[129] Darko and Snodderly (eds), 14.

[130] C H Dodd, *The Parables of the Kingdom*, (London: Nisbet, 1935), 50.

[131] Ken R Gnanakan, *Kingdom Concerns: A Biblical Exploration Towards a Theology of Mission*, (Bangalore, India: Theological Book Trust, 1989), 109.

[132] J D G Dunn, "Pentecost," in C Brown (ed), *New International Dictionary of the New Testament*, (Exeter: Paternoster, 1976), 783-88.

the narrow door." Many will be thrown out due to their evil doing. It shows the importance of leading a Christian life, honoring the Lord and King in the present. "People will come from East and West, North and South, and will take their places at the feast in the Kingdom of God" (Luke 13:29). The horizon of the future Kingdom influences the horizon of the present to make the church the Kingdom community. Church is not the Kingdom of God but is the result of the preaching of the Kingdom of God, the fellowship of those who have experienced the power and tasted the blessings of the Kingdom. The focus of the message which the early Church communicated to Jews (Luke 10:9), to Samaritans (Acts 8:12), and to everyone (28:31) was the Kingdom of God. Jesus proclaimed the Kingdom, and the Church's task is to preach Christ as did the early Church. To preach Christ is to proclaim the Kingdom in which Christ is the Lord. New Testament Gospel is the Gospel of the Kingdom which is the good news of God's reign of righteousness, peace, and salvation. The Gospel writers refer indiscriminately to the Gospel as the Gospel of the Kingdom (Matt. 4:23, 24:14, Mark 1:15, Luke 8:1, Acts 10:36), whereas, Paul had distinctive terms: a Gospel of salvation (Eph. 1:13, Rom. 1:16), a Gospel of peace (Rom. 10:15, Eph. 6:15), a Gospel of grace (Acts 20:24), and by implication, a Gospel of righteousness (Matt. 6:33, Rom. 14:17). Luke concluded Acts of the Apostles with the remarkable statement about the apostle, "boldly and without hindrance he preached the kingdom of God and taught about the Lord Jesus Christ" (Acts 28:31). William Shenk writes,

the Gospel is not to be treated lightly. It is not the possession of the Church. The Church itself was created by the Gospel and can remain true to its calling only by sharing the Gospel of the Kingdom with others, for the King's message is for all the people. The Church experiences its most vital solidarity with the King when carrying out the King's wishes.[133]

The Gospel of Matthew makes it clear that Christ's coming was a threat to the established kingdoms of the earth. He was heralded as a King at birth (2:2). He made the Kingdom of God His message (4:17) and called it the good news – the Gospel (4:23, Luke 4:43). The fervent prayer of the church is always, "Thy kingdom come, Thy will be done on earth as it is in heaven" (Matt. 6:10). There is nothing more awesome than to be assured in our hearts that we labor for the sake of the Kingdom, to make God's glory known. It is this Kingdom perspective that helps us to work effectively with people from different backgrounds and cultures.[134]

Summary

This chapter deals with the foundation and focus of Spirit-anointed witness in holistic Christian Mission. Christ-event is viewed as the divine intervention in history through the person and work of Christ for the reconciliation of humanity to God. It was not accidental, rather the fulfillment of the predestined plan of God. The focus of the witness is the Kingdom of God. This chapter reflects a common assumption that theological reflection on the church's Mission and ministry need to be grounded in Jesus' theology of the Kingdom of God. The church is not the Kingdom but witness of the Kingdom which is God's action and gift. We stand as an eschatological community with the right focus in life, the Kingdom of God.

---

[133] Shenk (ed), 103.
[134] Saji Lukos, Kingdom Perspective: Lessons Learned to Impact Our World, (Huntley IL: Mall Publishing, 2016), 132.

CHAPTER 4
DYNAMIC OF THE SPIRIT-ANOINTED WITNESS: SPIRIT-ANOINTING

Introduction

Spirit-anointing is debated among Christian thinkers regarding the dynamic of Christian witness. There are some who reckon it is the love of Christ which compels, and, others align themselves with scripture, the written Word. Classic Pentecostals favor the term "Spirit-baptism," with speaking in tongues an initial sign as a dynamic for the mission; unfortunately, this excludes some who are passionately engaged in mission and are greatly used by the Lord. However, in the researcher's perspective, Spirit-anointing is a distinctive authorizing, empowering, and equipping experience to carry out a specific divine assignment, which is evidenced in one's commitment, consistency, courage, confidence, passion, and stewardship in life and witness. Spirit-baptism is for enjoining a person with the body of Christ to realize the oneness and unity which is also a distinctive experience subsequent to regeneration. The doctrine of anointing has been associated with the fullness of the Spirit. There is, however, a difference between them as well. God anointed Jesus of Nazareth with the Holy Spirit and power: He preached the good news of peace, went around doing good, and healed those who were under the power of the devil. The anointing and fullness upon Jesus resulted in holistic mission (Acts 10:37-38).

Holy Spirit in Trinity

The Holy Spirit was certainly the experience of the community long before Pneumatology was developed. We need a proper theological understanding of the Spirit and Trinity with a relational emphasis in missiology too. Stanley Samartha, an Indian theologian, writes,

To most Christians, the Holy Spirit is associated not so much with doctrine as with life. It is in the unwrapping of the gift of God in Jesus Christ that the Spirit becomes alive in the hearts and minds of Christians. The Spirit inwardly nourishes the new life in Christ and guides the community of believers in their acts of witness and service in the world. The Spirit makes the *koinonia* in Christ real to the believers.[135]

There have been heretical views of the Spirit as there are heretical views of Christ all these years. One of them is, the Holy Spirit cannot be said to be God in the same way as Father and the Son. The statement at the council of Nicaea is very short on the third person of the Trinity, and managed to affirm only, "we believe in the Holy Spirit." The council of Constantinople (381) dogmatized the deity of the Spirit in its formulation "the Lord and Giver of Life Who proceedeth from the Father, Who with the Father and the Son together is worshipped and glorified."[136] Veli-Matti Karkkainen quotes Augustine's definition on the Spirit, "Holy Spirit is neither the Father nor the Son, but only the Spirit of the Father and of the Son, Himself also co-equal with the Father and the Son, and pertaining to the unity of the Trinity."[137] The Father, the Son, and the Holy Spirit are each distinct from one another, each spoken of as personal, and also spoken of as One. All these truths are believed on the evidence of Scripture, by which the doctrine of the Trinity is formed.

The Deity and Personality of the Holy Spirit

The deity of the Holy Spirit is His association with the Father and Son on a basis of apparent equality. The best evidences are found in the baptismal formula (Matt. 28:19), and the Pauline benediction (2 Cor. 13:14). Three members of the Godhead are linked in discussion on spiritual gifts by Paul (1 Cor. 12:4-6), and in the respective roles in the process of salvation by Peter (1 Pet. 1:2).

The first evidence of the Spirit's personality is the use of the masculine pronoun in representing Him. As Jesus describes the Holy Spirit's ministry (John 16:13-14), He uses the masculine pronoun, *ekeinos* (Gk). The term *paracletos* is applied to the Holy Spirit in John 14:16-17, 26, and 15:26. It is obvious that it is not some sort of abstract influence which is in view; Jesus is also expressly spoken of as a *parakletos* (1 John 2:1). In addition, Jesus said, He would pray to the Father, Who would give the disciples another *paracletos*. The word for "another" here is "*allos*" which means "another of the same kind." Jesus says that "the Holy Spirit will glorify Me for He will take what is Mine and declare it to you" (John 16:14). We find the parallel in the high-priestly prayer of Jesus: He states that during His earthly ministry on earth He glorified the Father (John 17:4). The Holy Spirit is also linked with the Father and the Son in various events of Jesus' ministry, one occurrence is at the time of baptism (Matt. 3:16-17).

The Holy Spirit can also be affected as a person. It is possible to lie to the Holy Spirit, as Ananias and Sapphira did (Acts 5:3-4), grieving the Holy Spirit (Eph. 4:30), and quenching the Spirit (1 Thess. 5:19), resisting the Holy Spirit (Acts 7:51), sin of blasphemy against the Holy Spirit (Matt. 12:31, Mark 3:29). The Holy Spirit also engaged in ministries which can be performed only by a person. They are teaching, regenerating, searching, speaking, interceding, commanding, testifying, guiding,

---

[135] Stanley J Samartha, "The Holy Spirit and People of Other Faiths," *Ecumenical Review* 42.3-4 (1990), 250-263.

[136] Gary D Badcock, "Holy Spirit, Doctrine," in Kevin J Vanhoozer, *Dictionary for Theological Interpretation of the Bible*, (Grand Rapids, MI: Baker Academic, 2005), 304.

[137] Veli-Matti Karkkainen, "Holy Spirit and the Doctrine of Trinity," in Johnson T K Lim (ed), *Holy Spirit: Unfinished Agenda*, (Singapore: Genesis Books and Word N Works, 2015), 127.

illuminating, and revealing. There are several other proofs to support that the Holy Spirit is a person, not a force, and that person is God.[138]

Jesus Christ inaugurated a new era. The risen Lord bestowed the Spirit on His disciples to prepare and equip them for their work as apostles among the nations. They were called to be witnesses among the people, sharing the good news of God's work in Christ. The last days arrived in the coming of Christ and in the descending of the Holy Spirit. The last days are the days of the Spirit, mission, and Church. These three cannot be separated; they belong together. A broadening of horizon takes place for a small group of disciples. From the Kingdom restored to Israel (Acts 1:6), attention is shifted to the ends of the earth (1:8). The interim period between incarnation and *Parousia* is the time when people are invited to move in the direction of the Kingdom of God, to move toward God in reconciliation, and toward each other in a new community of faith, love, and hope.

The disciples were called to be witnesses among the nations; however, they were weak and failed to act in the right way at the close of Jesus' earthly ministry. They were not depicted as heroes of faith. Luke describes in the last chapter of his Gospel the disappointment and despair, the confusion and doubt of the disciples because of what happened to their Master. They were expected to continue the mission entrusted by Him to them. Here, Mission starts with waiting. They had to wait for the coming of the Holy Spirit, the power from on high (Luke 24:49). "The emphasis on waiting leaves no room for human triumphalism. There is only room for grateful surprise that the Spirit of God is not ashamed to use weak, failing instruments – the surprise of grace."[139]

Historical Significance

The promise of Christ was initially fulfilled on the day of Pentecost. Pentecost was originally a harvest festival, a festival of weeks (Exod. 23:16, 34:22), the festival of first fruits. The coming of the Holy Spirit is the beginning of the harvest, the gathering of the new humanity. Later Pentecost became a festival in memory of the receiving of the Law at Mt Sinai at the day of assembly (Deut. 4:10, 9:10, 10:4). The new Pentecost also has universal meaning. The good news of God's saving act is heard in different languages. The Holy Spirit crosses boundaries and the Gospel is translatable.

Another link from the Old Testament is Genesis 11 which tells us how descendants of Noah tried to stay together and make a name for themselves by building a city with a tower reaching into the heavens. It resulted in division and confusion. We read in Acts 2 the initiatory role of the Holy Spirit to overcome division and confusion by creating a new community in the Spirit.

The Promised Gift

The gift of the Holy Spirit is technically called the "promise of the Father." It was not only promised by Jesus, but by prophets in the Old Testament. The promise of God given in Ezekiel 36:26-27 is fulfilled in the New Testament experience of regeneration. The promise of Joel 2:28-29 is fulfilled in the Pentecostal experience, according to Peter (Acts 2:14ff). John the Baptist, in defining the ministry of the Messiah, declared, "He shall baptize you with the Holy Spirit" (Matt. 3:11). It is inferred from the Scripture that God the Father, Son, and the Holy Spirit made a covenant of redemption

---

[138] Erickson, 862.
[139] Shenk, 113.

between them even before the foundations of the World which involved the work of the various persons in the Trinity in historical time. The references to the covenant are mentioned in the Bible: your name written in the Lamb's book of life from before the foundations of the World, the Lamb slain from before the foundations of the World, the Kingdom prepared from before the foundations of the World. These references could be made only on the ground of a plan of God which had been purposed from eternity. Since God foreknew the fall of man and the separation between God and man through sin, His plan of redemption was to restore His fellowship and His dwelling with men. Now, God dwells in the Church by the Holy Spirit (Eph. 2:22). The fulfillment of the Lord's plan to dwell with His people came in the outpouring of the Holy Spirit and by the filling of the Spirit in individual believers.

The Necessity of Pentecost

Pentecost-event fulfilled the disciples' expectation of what Jesus had promised: God became near, a reality, a mighty force in their lives. "Why Pentecost?" must be answered theologically, historically, and individually. Only by these answers are we able to see the necessity of Pentecost[140]

A. Theologically, Pentecost was necessary to complete the divine part in redemption. God the Father planned, foreordained, predestined, and elected events. Salvation originated in the love and wisdom of God the Father. God the Son, by incarnation, assumed human flesh and perfect human nature so as to obey the divine plan and to bear the penalty of sin by making atonement for it. God the Holy Spirit effectively applied this redemption unto men by regenerating them and making real the benefits of redemption. The outpouring of the Holy Spirit occurred in history, and needs to be activated in our lives. Everyone who believes in Christ shouldn't assume that the Spirit is empowering, rather, each needs to experience it personally through faith, prayer, and waiting in His presence. It is evidenced in power and authority. Christian historian Kenneth Scott Latourette says that "the coming of the Holy Spirit was of major importance because it changed the believers into enthusiastic witnesses of Christ."[141]

B. Historically, Pentecost was necessary to give a factual basis to faith. The Crucifixion of Jesus on Calvary is a fact which occurred in a definite time and place. This provides us a secure foundation for our belief. Similarly, the resurrection of Jesus Christ is a historical fact. In this event, the supernatural occurred in a demonstrable way. In the same way, the fact of Pentecost is a historical event which makes the Church dynamic in this World. The failure of the church at present is the theory formulated that once the Spirit came historically at Pentecost, it was not necessary to personally receive the Spirit's empowerment in one's life. This subject is to be addressed logically too. Because Christ died on the cross and was resurrected, do we assume that salvation has become our individual experience? It is to be activated through personal confession of faith and repentance from our sins. Joy of salvation and assurance is the result of believing in Christ. Though Pentecost occurred in history, it needs to be activated in our specific lives. Everyone who believes in Christ shouldn't assume that the Spirit is empowering, rather, the individual will receive empowerment personally through faith, prayer, and waiting in His presence.

C. Individually, Pentecost was necessary to guarantee the blessings of God to all men. The Holy Spirit is God's gift to the repentant believing sinner (Acts 2:38). The blessings are declared by Paul,

[140] Harold John Ockenga, *Power Through Pentecost,* (Grand Rapids: Eerdmans Publishing, 1959), 18-20.
[141] Kenneth Scott Latourette, *A History of Christianity,* (Peabody, MA: Prince Press, 2000), 59.

"Praise be to the God and Father of Jesus Christ Who has blessed us in the heavenly realms with every spiritual blessing in Christ" (Eph. 1:3). This may be translated by the "Spirit blessings." In the wake of the Spirit comes every desirable gift of God. Wisdom and power come through the Holy Spirit.

We believe that God is pouring out His Spirit on Christians throughout the World. The Prophet Joel announced it hundreds of years before Christ, "In the last days, God says, I will pour out My Spirit on all people. Your sons and daughters will prophesy, your young men will see visions, your old men will dream dreams" (Acts 2:17). Peter continued, "the promise is for you and your children and for all who are far off – for all whom the Lord our God will call" (2:39). There are three groups of people in Christian Churches. The first equate the conversion experience with fulfillment of the outpouring of the Spirit in life. The second consider Spirit baptism as a second blessing which is a synonym for spirit anointing and spirit filling. The third group are confused about the Person and work of the Holy Spirit because of division and confusion in the Church. We come across people who appreciate the vibrancy of spirituality with openness to the experience and activity of the Spirit in Church and personal life. A Scriptural foundation is needed for understanding and experience.

Development of the Doctrine and Experience of the Spirit

Development of the doctrine and experience of the Spirit has been varied throughout the centuries. Representatives of the Catholic tradition held in common their conviction that the Spirit was given in the sacraments of the Church, yet they were divided over the question of whether there was one anointing or two.[142] The passages in Acts of the Apostles on "the Sprit is poured out" with the promise of the "gift of the Spirit" in John 14-16 relate to Paul's comment on "being sealed by the Spirit" in Ephesians 1:13. It is suggested that the recipients in all these cases were regenerate, that is, they were already born of the Spirit. Robert S Rayburn writes in "Baptism of the Holy Spirit and the Second Blessing,"

In the last 30 years the subject has most often been discussed in terms of the Pentecostal or Charismatic view of the second blessing, an experience marked by tongues – speaking and the like but, the general idea is old as Montanism, a Christian sect of the 2nd and 3rd Centuries and has been found throughout Christian history in many different forms.[143]

John Wesley developed a theory that the work of sanctification as well as justification is instantaneous. The remission of sins and new heart are two distinct moments in the life of a Christian. So, Wesley preveniently shaped the Pentecostal understanding of a crisis and conscious experience of the baptism of the Holy Spirit subsequent to conversion. While theologically Methodism exerted the major influence, methodologically, American revivalism under the leadership of Charles Finney and D L Moody, at the beginning and at the end of the 19th Century moved further for Spirit-filled

---

[142] Chad Owen Brand (ed), *Perspectives on Spirit Baptism: Five Views*, (Nashville: B&H Academic, 2004), 10.
[143] Robert Rayburn, "Baptism of the Holy Spirit and the Second Blessing," http://reformedperspectives.org/articles/rob_rayburn/rob_rayburn.Acts19.1_7.html (Accessed December 15, 2017).

experience. "Inheriting Wesley's experiential theology and Revivalism's experiential methodology, Pentecostalism went out into an experience-hungry world and found response."[144]

Teachings on the Holy Spirit, particularly of A J Gordon, F B Meyer, A B Simpson, Andrew Murray and R A Torrey – all rather prominent figures in the English-speaking evangelical World – have impacted greatly the emergence of a theology of mission with the empowering function of the Holy Spirit. The Keswick movement and its doctrine of "the Higher Life" ignited the passion for a distinctive experience. "A B Simpson, Hannah Whitehall Smith, and others believed in a filling of the Holy Spirit that occurred and left a permanent change when one gave oneself up to God more fully than one had or could at his or her conversion, leading in some cases to complete freedom from known sin."[145]

Frank Macchia contends that "Spirit Baptism" should be the crown jewel of Pentecostal distinctive. Further, such a focus will enable Pentecostals to better contribute toward healthier ecumenism among the Churches while simultaneously challenging other Christian traditions concerning aspects of the experience of the Spirit.[146]

Is Baptism in the Spirit a mere Pentecostal Theology? It is not, and people of different traditions in Christianity uphold this doctrine with various interpretations. The Reformed Tradition defends the position: it tends to see initial conversion includes baptism in/with the Spirit or bestowal of the Spirit. Classical Pentecostalism holds the position that baptism in the Spirit is distinct and subsequent to the conversion experience, which is evidenced by speaking in tongues. It is linked with empowerment for prophetic witness. This position is a hindrance for a united Christ-centered witness everywhere. Baptism in the Spirit is a single act of uniting a believer unto the living organism of the Church to realize the unity and oneness of the body of Christ (1 Cor. 12:13). It is a matter of position rather than power. The anointing of the Holy Spirit is an authorizing and empowering act of God with the purpose of witnessing Christ (Luke 4:18-19, Acts 1:8, 10:38). The fact that both occurred simultaneously on the day of Pentecost doesn't guarantee this for all in a single occasion now. The reason for the position is that many who claimed to have baptism in the Holy Spirit at conversion or as an experience subsequent to conversion do not have any passion or commitment for Christian witness. They are content either with traditional biased frozen spirituality or with charismatic worship. What is truly lacking in them is the anointing for witness. The significance of anointing is to be restored in life and practice.

Jesus Christ wanted His disciples to stay in the city until they had been endowed with power from on high because they were weak and fearful in carrying out the mission which was critical on occasions after Jesus was apprehended by the officials and even after His resurrection. Natural abilities were not enough to fulfill their call and commitment. They needed to be authorized, empowered, and equipped by a supernatural intervention. This was not optional but mandatory for the disciples as Jesus repeated the command immediately before His ascension (Acts 1:4). We are enlightened to know that we are involved in a fully authorized task with a spiritual dynamic that gives us confidence, boldness, and a sense of legitimate freedom in Christian witness.

---

[144] Frederick Dale Brunner, A Theology of the Holy Spirit: The Pentecostal Experience and the New Testament Witness, (Eugene, OR: Wipf and Stock Publishers, 1997), 39.
[145] Rayburn, "Baptism," (Accessed December 15, 2017).
[146] Frank Macchia, in Peter D Neumann, *Pentecostal Experience: An Ecumenical Encounter*, (Eugene, OR: Pickwick Publications, 2012), 169.

There is general agreement that the gift of the Holy Spirit in Acts is above all a prophetic empowerment to witness of Jesus Christ. This has usually been interpreted in one of the two ways,

Scholars in the classical Pentecostal tradition like Stronstad and Menzies have inclined to argue that Luke understands the Pentecostal gift to the disciples in Parallel to Jesus' Jordan experience, and so exclusively as a *donum superadditum* empowering mission (Luke 4:18-21, 24:47-49, Acts 1:8, 2:11). This Pentecostal experience of the disciples has been then taken as paradigmatic for all believers. Secondly, scholars like Haya Prats and Mainville have argued for a charismatic endowment serving more wide-ranging (including ecclesiastically orientated) ends.[147]

However, it is reasonable to integrate both views for a realistic approach in theology and missiology. The church is set apart for sanctified life and to witness of Jesus Christ as Lord and Savior of the World.

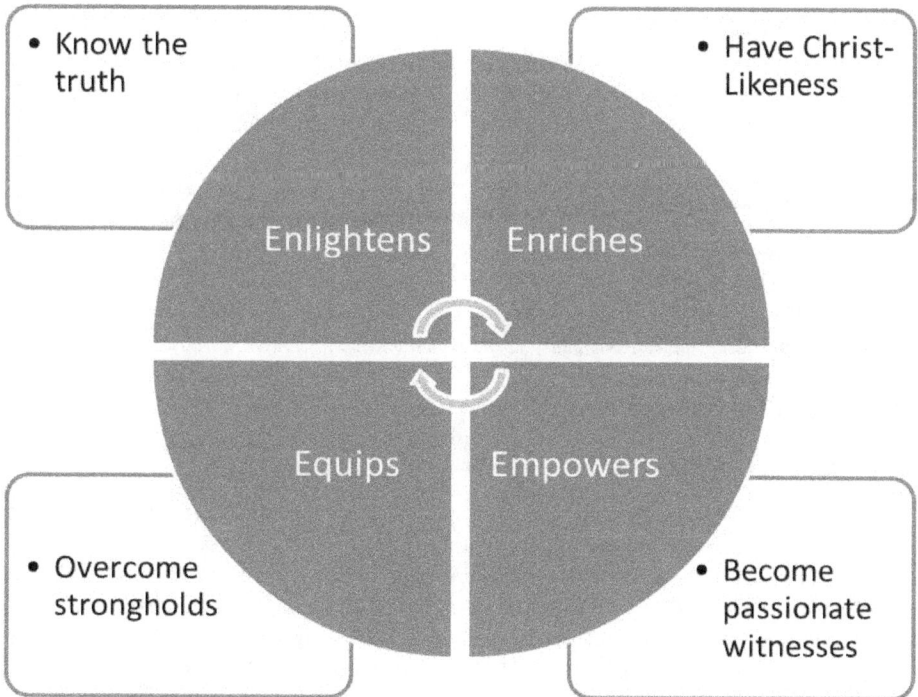

Figure 4: The Spirit-anointing: Purpose

The Anointing Enlightens Us to Know the Truth (John 14:14-16)

The disciples of Jesus Christ were instructed to believe and hold to His teaching because the truth would set them free (John 8:31-32). Satan attempts to blind the eyes of people to the Word of God, to

---

147 Turner, The Holy Spirit and Spiritual Gifts, 46.

doubt the Word, and to withhold them from the truth. Jesus assured the disciples before departing the World that the Spirit of truth would be with them forever (14:15-16). The anointing remains in us to teach us in all situations and about all things (1 John 2:26-27). There have been controversies on formulations of faith throughout the Centuries, churches divided, persecutions occurred, and many became martyrs for holding to the truth. Conversely there have been many who have stood firm for the truth despite challenges.

The Anointing Enriches Us to have Christ-Likeness (Phil. 2:5)

Christ-likeness is the primary manifestation of the anointing. The focus is totally upon what God desires and what God has willed. God showers His surrendered children with His awesome love by the Spirit (Rom. 5:5). Through the Power we are transformed into His likeness. Our attitude should be same as that of Christ Jesus (Phil. 2:5).

We could have the mind of Christ as a spiritual exercise. It is the most powerful force in the world. Once we have received God's love into our lives, its power enables us to live fully for Him. We find ourselves both eager and able to live out His promise to us of a joyous life of service as we engage in the task of building His kingdom. The bestowing of God's love is always followed by God's command that we bestow that love on others.[148]

The Son in His glory yielded to the will of the Father to step down to earth for accomplishing an act of love (Heb. 10:7). This prayer of Jesus is beautifully presented in Scripture as an example for us. "Christ-likeness involves a basic love of doing the will of God which could, in a given instance, be demonstrated in an act which on the surface seems to be unkind."[149] We are called to follow the steps of Christ Who showed the example (1 Pet. 2:21-25). The church is privileged with the anointed ministers, apostles, prophets, evangelists, pastors and teachers, with the purpose that the body of Christ may be built up to reach unity in the faith and in the knowledge of the Son of God, and become mature, attaining to the whole measure of the fullness of Christ (Eph. 4:11-13).

The Anointing empowers us to have a Passionate Witness (Acts 1:8)

Threats and challenges from the religious, social, or political realm couldn't distract the minds of the early disciples because of the anointing by which they were known, the purpose for which they were set apart in life. The testimony of Jesus before Pilate remains unique (John 18:37). The boldness of Peter in preaching "Christ crucified and risen" in Acts 2 is a vivid example. He spoke to the Sanhedrin (4:8) with confidence though he was warned by the religious authority. The testimony of Peter representing other disciples stands above any other accounts in Acts, "we will obey God not men" (Acts 4:19-20, 5:29). The disciples of Jesus Christ are expected to demonstrate absolute loyalty to Him for the higher calling and anointing. Robert P Menzies describes it as "the prophetic anointing which enables them to participate effectively in the missionary enterprise of the church."[150] Acts of the Apostles describes how the disciples witnessed with the gifts of the Spirit: demonstrated in faith,

[148] Tom Paterson, Deeper, Richer, Fuller: Discover the Spiritual Life You Long For, (New York: Howard Books, 2010), 227-228.
[149] Charles Ryrie, *Balancing the Christian Life*, (Chicago: Moody Publishers, 1994), 123.
[150] Robert P Menzies, "The Spirit Baptism and Spiritual Gifts," in *Pentecostalism in Context: Essays in Honor of William W Menzies*, (Sheffield, UK: Sheffield Academic Press, 1997), 53-54.

word of wisdom, prophesy, tongues, healing, discerning, casting out demons, and so on. The apostles developed the understanding, significance, purpose, and use of gifts in Christian ministry (Rom. 12:4-8, 1 Cor. 12:4-11, Eph. 4:11-12, 1 Pet. 4:7-11, 1 Tim. 4:14).

A spiritual gift is a supernatural capacity or power bestowed on a Christian by the Holy Spirit to enable that person to exercise his or her function as a member of the body of Christ. These gifts are not to be thought of as natural abilities nor are permanent possessions, rather, the gifts are supernatural manifestations of the Spirit Himself. John Rea describes the importance of gifted ministry by the Church with scriptural support.[151] There are many reasons for the continuing manifestation of gifts of the Holy Spirit from the first century until now. First, the gifts manifest the power of God in the body of Christ on earth. God's purpose is to confound all mere worldly wisdom (1 Cor. 1:27, 2:6-10). That is why Paul was led to repudiate his training in Judaism and his natural advantages (1 Cor. 2:1-5, Phil. 3:3-8) and to tell only what Christ had accomplished through him in the power of signs and wonders (Rom. 15:18-19). Second, the gifts edify and perfect the Church. Third, the gifts aid in carrying out the Great Commission. Jesus Christ promised before the ascension that supernatural signs would give confirmation to the Gospel wherever His believers would go to preach it (Mark 16:9-20). The apostles combated heathenism, not by convincing oratory and superior education, rather by gifts of healing and miracle (Acts 14:8-18, 16:16-18, 19:11-20, 28:1-10). Fourth, the gifts effect the deliverance of the people. Jesus was anointed to preach the Gospel to the poor and proclaim deliverance to the captives. Mathew Vargheese writes,

The church is a charismatic community. There are different gifts of the Spirit (1 Cor. 12:4-6), and each is important for the whole function of the Church. Therefore, the question, which one of the gifts is more important, is irrelevant. It is the proper use of them in love and mutual submission that the gifts are most useful within the community.[152]

Gifts are bestowed upon the Church as a stewardship for His glory. We too need to be authorized, equipped, and empowered to carry out His work now, to rescue the lost from the grip of Satan and his power (Acts 26:18). Through the ministry of Philip at Samaria, many who had unclean spirits were set free (Acts 8:5-7). By the gift of the discerning Spirit, we may detect the unseen foe and expose the dark angel of light (2 Cor. 2:11, 11:13-14), as Peter did regarding Ananias (Acts 5:1-11). God's purpose in bestowing Spiritual gifts is that through their operation Christians might witness of Christ with more confidence and power. So, the Spirit-anointing is a significant distinct experience to carry out a specific divine assignment which is evidenced in one's commitment, consistency, courage, confidence, and zeal with faithfulness and stewardship in life and witness. It is relational, vertically and horizontally.

Summary

The Holy Spirit is affirmed as a person in the Godhead Who functions relationally. The Spirit-event on the day of Pentecost was the dynamic of Christian witness. Spirit-anointing becomes a necessity for all because it is a distinct authorizing experience subsequent to conversion or baptism.

---

[151] John Rea, *The Holy Spirit in the Bible: A Commentary*, (Lake Mary, FL: Creation House, 1990), 245-46.
[152] Mathew C Vargheese, "Christian Theology as Pneumatic Praxis," in M Stephen (ed), *Faith and Praxis: Essays and Reflections in Honor of Rev Dr T G Koshy*, (Manakala, Kerala, India: Faith Theological Seminary, 2012), 91.

It enlightens us to know the truth, enriches us to have Christ-likeness, empowers us to become passionate witnesses, and equips us to overcome strongholds in life and ministry. Anointing in the Spirit comes upon an individual by God which enables one to carry out mission with faithfulness and integrity. The spiritual anointing sets apart a person's heart and mind with love, truth, and the missional call of God to ministry.

CHAPTER 5
MESSAGE AND METHOD

Introduction
The core message of Christian mission is the message of salvation by the grace of God accomplished through the reconciliatory act of Jesus Christ. To become a witness of Christ one must primarily know Jesus Christ: The Person, words, and deeds. Methods in Christian witness derive from Scripture: the text and the context. Jesus Christ, the early apostles, and missionaries throughout the centuries employed several methods to be effective in the task.

Message: Reconciliation
The most characteristic meaning of salvation in Scripture is expressed in the language of reconciliation and peace. Humanity's alienation and hostility toward God and each other causes self-destruction. The wage of sin is death (Rom. 6:23). But God's gracious act of forgiveness and reconciliation saves from destruction and restores the possibility of eternal life in fellowship with Himself. Paul is the only New Testament writer who uses the language of reconciliation (the Greek verb *katallasso* – to reconcile, and the noun form *katallage* – reconciliation). The foremost use of the idea of reconciliation has God as its object (2 Cor. 5:18-21). So, man doesn't affect any change in his relationship by any merit on his part to persuade God to respond with such favor. God initiated the foundation upon which reconciliation becomes attainable while we were opposed to God.

Historical Development of the Message

It was Athanasius (ca. AD 297-373) who first developed the idea of the inextricable relationship between the incarnation and atonement. For him soteriology was the pervading influence of the biblical revelation. He maintained that,
man had lost the life of God, thereby bringing upon himself the process of decay, pollution, and a progressive diminishing of the image and knowledge of God. He argued that the only solution for the Creator was to take it upon Himself to effect man's reconciliation. The essence of God's being dictated that this could only be viable by Him taking human flesh, revealing Himself as the Savior of mankind, and executing the penalty for sin in righteous judgement by bearing the shame of the cross, and proclaiming its victory in the power of the resurrection. In later years, Athanasius revised his concept

of the *Theanthropos* considerably. While sustaining the prominence of the absolute necessity and inseparability of the incarnation and atonement, he further reinforced the notion that reconciliation took place initially within the person of the Christ, or more specifically, in the hypostatical union of the two natures of Christ.[153]

Anselm of Canterbury (1033 – 1109) expressed the role of the *Theanthropos* in redemption history. The emphasis was more annexed to the divine satisfaction against the sins of humanity. T F Torrance insists that this reconciliation is achieved in the person of the incarnate Son, Jesus Christ. "It is a work of His Person, which is inseparable from His Person, and is to be found only within His Person, in the inseparable unity of His Person and work."[154] For some others, reconciliation becomes first of all attainable by the life of Christ as much as by His death and then, by extension, possible also by a life lived in accordance with the example Jesus set, without any necessity to initially embrace the atoning work of His death and resurrection. But we cannot subscribe to this development of doctrine, which is a deviation from the core of the Christian message. Chris Woodall states his conviction, "the reconciliation without repentance is anathema to the biblical revelation of both concepts. Moreover, sanctification that fails to acknowledge salvation as its gateway is wholly unattainable by us."[155]

John Stott identifies four images of salvation: Propitiation, redemption, justification, and reconciliation. In reflecting on this he writes,

reconciliation is probably the most popular of the four because, it is the most personal. We have left behind the temple precincts (Propitiation), the slave market (Redemption), and the law courts (Justification); we are now in our home with our family and friends. True, there is a quarrel, even "enmity," but "to reconcile" means to restore a relationship, to renew a friendship. So, an original relationship is presupposed which, having been broken, has been recovered by Christ.[156]

Pauline Teaching on Reconciliation

There are four major conciliatory passages (Rom. 5:10-11, Eph. 2:11-22, Col. 1:19-23, 2 Cor. 5:18-21). Paul's common approach is to suggest an act of putting right a relationship that had previously been one of acrimony and antagonism. The cause of our impaired relationship is sin and the basis for its restoration is the effective management of that problem. Hence, "Christ died for our sins" (1 Cor. 15:3). Based on this theme, reconciliation, D Martyn Lloyd-Jones draws the following conclusions:

a. It means...a change from a hostile to a friendly relationship.
b. It doesn't merely mean a friendship after an estrangement...It means really bringing together again, a reuniting, a reconnecting.
c. It is a word also that emphasizes the completeness of the action. It is not a compromise...it is a complete action which produces complete unity and accord where there was formerly hostility.
d. This word that the apostle uses implies that it is one of the parties that takes the action, and it is the upper one that takes it...it suggests an action that comes down from above.

---

[153] Athanasius, in Chris Woodall, *Atonement: God's Means of Effecting Man's Reconciliation*, (Eugene, OR: Wipf and Stock 2015), 88.
[154] Thomas F Torrance, *Atonement: The Person and Work of Christ*, (Downers Grove, IL: IVP Academic, 2009), xiv.
[155] Woodall, 89.
[156] John Stott, *The Cross of Christ*, (Leicester, UK: InterVarsity, 2006), 192.

e.   The word carries the meaning that it is a restoration of something that was there before...They were conciled (estranged) before; they are now reconciled, brought back to where they were.[157]

Salvation is described as the peace (*Shalom*) of God that flows from God's forgiveness and reconciliation. In Romans 5:1-11, the emphasis is upon the reconciliation between individual and God – peace with God. Paul writes, we are justified, reconciled, and saved from the wrath of God through the death and resurrection of Jesus Christ. Reconciliation involves the removal of the enmity of the one offended by sin. By the atoning death of Christ, God is reconciled to us. His grace and justice are a harmonious whole. Our personal reconciliation, our turning from enmity to love God, is grounded on the decisive act of God in removing the enmity on His side. There is a parallelism between reconciliation (verse 10) and justification (verse 9). Paul regards justification here as a change of status, as forensic, as restoration to the favor of God. Reconciliation is seen as a gift (verse 11), which is objective in nature, rather than a subjective change in human beings.[158]

Paul locates our reconciliation to God at the point of Christ's death, and looks forward to its ultimate consummation when Christ returns. You who were far away have been brought near through the blood of Christ (Eph. 2:13). Those who had been aliens are included in the covenant of promise and have been made fellow citizens and members of the household of God. This new standing in God's sight and purpose marks the possibility of a new reconciled community where the old walls of discrimination and hostility are broken down. Here, the nationalistic features of personhood are dropped and those who are reconciled are a community of people who share one life and purpose in Christ (Acts 4:32). Their new identity as the family of God through Jesus Christ (Eph. 2:19), or their new allegiance to the Kingdom of God and His righteousness (Matt. 6:33), restores that social unity and transcendent purpose which gives human existence its true dignity and worth (Gal. 3:26-28).[159]

In Colossians 1:19-20, reconciliation is seen to encompass the final renovation of the entire cosmos, but, it is still the death of Christ that is its basis: "for God was pleased to have all His fullness dwell in Him, and through Him to reconcile to Himself all things, whether things on earth or things in heaven, by making peace through His blood shed on the cross." The Colossians had a flawed cosmology in which angelic spirits played the role of mediators between God and human beings and Christ was given an inferior position.

Paul the apostle was entrusted with the ministry of reconciliation. He acts as an ambassador of Christ urging his hearers to trust in Him. "All this is from God, Who reconciled us to Himself through Jesus Christ and gave us the ministry of reconciliation: that God was reconciling the world to Himself in Christ, not counting men's sin against them and He has committed to us the message of reconciliation. We are therefore Christ's ambassadors, as though God were making His appeal through us. We implore you on Christ's behalf: Be reconciled to God. God made Him Who had no sin to be sin for us, so that in Him we might become the righteousness of God" (2 Cor. 5:18-21). James Denney explicitly deals with the theme of reconciliation:

Just because the experience of reconciliation is the central and fundamental experience of the Christian religion, the doctrine of reconciliation is not so much one doctrine as the inspiration and

[157] D Martin Lloyd-Jones, *God's Way of Reconciliation: Ephesians 2:1-22*, (Edinburgh: Banner of Truth, 1981), 285.
[158] Robert Letham, *The Work of Christ: Contours of Christian Theology*, (Downers Grove: InterVarsity Press, 1993), 147.
[159] Norman C Kraus, *Missions, Evangelism, and Church Growth*, (Scottdale, PA: Herald Press, 1980), 73-74.

focus of all ... in the experience of reconciliation to God through Christ is to be found the principle and the touchstone of all genuine Christian doctrine.[160]

Christian faith and proclamation arise from God's gracious willingness to reveal Himself as Savior and draw us into a knowing communion with Himself. Jesus Christ is at once both the center of and the entry way into the doctrine of God. "No one knows the Son except the Father, and no one knows the Father except the Son and anyone to whom the Son chooses to reveal Him" (Matt. 11:27).

There is an ontological relation between the Father and the Son in being and act to be the sole ground of revelation and salvation. Thus, theology is a knowledge of the Father, through the Son, and in the unity of the Holy Spirit. Such theology is at all times thoroughly Trinitarian, for the knowledge of God is mediated through Jesus Christ, and therefore God is known through encounter, for God is Spirit.[161]

Our task is more rather than less faithful knowledge of God Who encounters us, with the end a right relationship with God and faithful living of the Christian life.

The story of Jesus' death and resurrection reveal the saving power of God. Theories of atonement attempt to provide a coherent explanation of Jesus' life, death, and resurrection. The theory of reconciliation calls for the restoration of the knowledge of God. The encounter with God always reveals a God Who stands over against our preferred views and personal longings for the sacred. God is sovereign, free, and uncontrollable. To know the sovereign God is to know God's promises and live in the expectation of their fulfillment. Human infidelity follows a familiar schema in the Old Testament: God is known, and commitments are made; there is a break in fidelity by human beings; a time of judgement occurs; the covenant is restored through human repentance and divine forgiveness. This cycle is repeated so often that in the book of Judges it becomes the story of each generation (Judges 2:10-15). The prophets continued to remind Israel of promises, infidelity and idolatry, followed by judgement and a call to repentance (Isa. 44:9-22, Jer. 3:6-14, Ezek. 14:5-8, Hos. 6:1-3, Amos 5:1-15). In this cycle of covenant making, breaking, and renewal, we see why restoration of the true knowledge of God involves atonement (Heb. 10:4-7, 13:20-21). The absence of true knowledge is not ignorance but idolatry and infidelity – as become evident in Israel's history. Therefore, finding the true knowledge of God always requires recognition, the knowledge that we have turned from God. Richard Niebuhr, in "Christ the Way to the Knowledge of God," writes, "Therefore, what is needed, is not mere instruction, but the restoration of our relation with God. This is more than an intellectual discovery; it is an act of spiritual transformation."[162]

The problem is that the true knowledge of God revealed in the creation has been lost because of human sin. Forsaking the true God, humankind has substituted the creation for the Creator. Consequently, human kind is characterized by idolatry and unable to discern the truth regarding God (Rom. 1:25). Jesus appears as the agent of God, revealing the truth about both God and humanity. He announces the rule of God and gathers a new covenant community that embodies life-giving knowledge. Entrance into the new community, however, can only occur through repentance (Mark

---

[160] James Denney, in Harold H Ditmanson, *Grace in Experience and Theology*, (Minneapolis: Augsburg Publishing House, 1977), 174.

[161] Andrew Purves, *Exploring Christology and Atonement*, (Downers Grove: IVP Academic, 2015), 22.

[162] Richard H Niebuhr, "Christ the Way to the Knowledge of God," in Peter Schmiechen, *Saving Power: Theories of Atonement and Forms of the Church*, (Grand Rapids: Eerdmans Publishing, 2005), 258.

1:15), wherein, one forsakes the idols of the World and trust in the false things of this World, including oneself.

Niebuhr introduces a threefold distinction for differentiating faith.[163] (1). Polytheism or pluralism recognizes many centers of value. It accepts the fact that trust and loyalty are distributed between many centers, producing inevitable disagreements, tensions, and conflicts. While those in the west associate religious polytheism with pre-modern cultures, Niebuhr uses this type to interpret the tensions of modern life, where multiple centers of value (the state, politics, economics, professions, corporations, family, race, gender) force people to choose between conflicting loyalties. (2). Henotheism is the attempt to make one of the many centers of value in the World into an absolute. It recognizes that others exist but demands trust and loyalty for only one. Henotheism, as the greatest threat to monotheism in the modern age, produces conflict because it is by nature divisive and oppressive. (3). Monotheism is the attempt to see all things unified in one center of value. To do this, two elements must be joined together. On the one hand, God, as the Source of all being and power, must be affirmed as good. It is Jesus and God Who are at the center. Among many human figures Jesus appears as the truly human. There is the trust and loyalty to God and to Jesus, whereby Jesus is called, baptized, anointed, and sent as God's messenger. In the end, it is God Who raises the crucified Lord. Though betrayed and abandoned by the disciples, God keeps the promise. "Jesus is revealed to possess the twofold status affirmed in the tradition of Chalcedon. The titles Father and Son are to be claimed as the final affirmations of God and Jesus. In the resurrection God is revealed as the faithful and trustworthy Father; Jesus is bestowed with power confirming His Sonship."[164] God's love and power are demonstrated in the Son's incarnation, death, and resurrection. The reconciliation and restoration of humanity are based on the above pillars of Christianity.

Repentance and Forgiveness

The message of Christianity is unique. The reconciliatory act of Jesus is evidenced in His incarnation, death, resurrection, exaltation, and the second coming of Christ. When Jesus proclaimed the good news of God and the Kingdom, repentance and faith were demanded from the hearers. Repentance in a heart demands taking a U-turn in life, recognizing that a person is headed in the wrong direction, and now turns in the right direction to reach the destiny. The confession of Zacchaeus is a model for all to realize that repentance is something that is to mark the whole life of the believer (Luke 19:8-10). It is transformational in making a bold decision for the correction in life. Peter's preaching on the day of Pentecost resulted in the repentance of 3000 people as a requirement for baptism, an outward expression of inward change (Acts 2:38). Jesus Christ opened the minds of the disciples that they could understand the scriptures (Luke 24:45). It is significant for everyone in following Christ to be the disciples of Christ. The Pauline prayer to the church at Ephesus, "that the eyes of your heart may be enlightened" (Eph. 1:17) is to be true with us to take heed to the instruction for waiting to be clothed with power from on high (Luke 24:49). The empowered disciples are commissioned with the message of repentance and forgiveness in the name of Jesus Christ. Vernon McGee writes, "Repentance means to turn back to Him and it is a message for the believers. How dare

163 Niebuhr, in Schmiechen, 264-65.
164 Schmiechen, 267.

the Church tell an unsaved man to repent."[165] What he needs to do is to turn to Christ for salvation. When he turns to Christ, he will turn from his sin – as the Thessalonians "...turned to God from idols to serve the living and true God; and to wait for His Son from heaven..." (1 Thess. 1:9-10). The messages to the churches in Revelation Chapters 2-3 include the action, "repent" (*metanoeson*, "a change of mind"). The churches in the present time need to pay attention to the warning and exhortation from the Spirit (Rev. 2:7, 3:6).

Forgiveness and reconciliation are vertical, as we experience them personally from God (Col. 1:14, 22). Gospel accounts narrate the authority of Jesus Christ to forgive sin (Luke 5:20, 7:48, John 8:11). Forgiveness and reconciliation are horizontal, as Jesus demanded this from all worshippers who come before the altar. Jesus said, "Therefore, if you are offering your gift at the altar, and there remember that your brother has something against you, leave your gift there in front of the altar. First, go and be reconciled to your brother; then come and offer your gift" (Matt. 5: 23-25, 6:12).

Method: Holistic Mission

Churches have traditional bindings while embracing methods in mission. The theological foundation and missionary methods are like two magnets. In every age, the church must be the magnet of methodology in proper alignment with the polarity of biblical orthodoxy. J D Payne writes,

the temptation is to allow our methods to shift with whims of societies and cultures to such a degree that context takes priority. Such should never be the case. The Bible is explicit on what is necessary for someone to enter the Kingdom of God: the nature of this God; the exclusivity of Christ's atoning work; and how a disciple should act in relation to his or her heavenly Father, other brothers and sisters, and those outside of the Kingdom.[166]

It is a challenge for the mission practitioners to find the right methods in mission in a changing World. Methods are to be renewed for effectiveness without leaving the message of the Gospel which needs courage from the missionaries. Payne writes,

as we consider missionary methods during our age, we should be asking questions such as, (A) Are our methods biblically grounded? (B) Are our methods ethical? (C) Do our methods avoid unhealthy pragmatism and paternalism? (D) Will our methods allow for the Gospel to connect with the people? (E) Are our methods highly reproducible among the people? (F) Do our teams have the necessary resources to use our methods?[167]

Jesus said that His kingdom was not of this World. This dimension of Christian faith has had many martyrs, led to asceticism, fired the zeal of missionary expansion, and created a burning eschatological hope. Jesus' example of selfless and compassionate service has set a pattern for ministry in all time.

---

[165] J Vernon McGee, *Revelation Chapters 1-5*, Thru the Bible Commentary Series, (Nashville: Thomas Nelson Publishers, 1991), 70.
[166] J D Payne, in Craig Ott and J D Payne (eds), *Missionary Methods: Research, Reflections, and Realities*, (Pasadena: William Carey Library, 2013), xviii.
[167] Payne, in Ott and Payne (eds), xix.

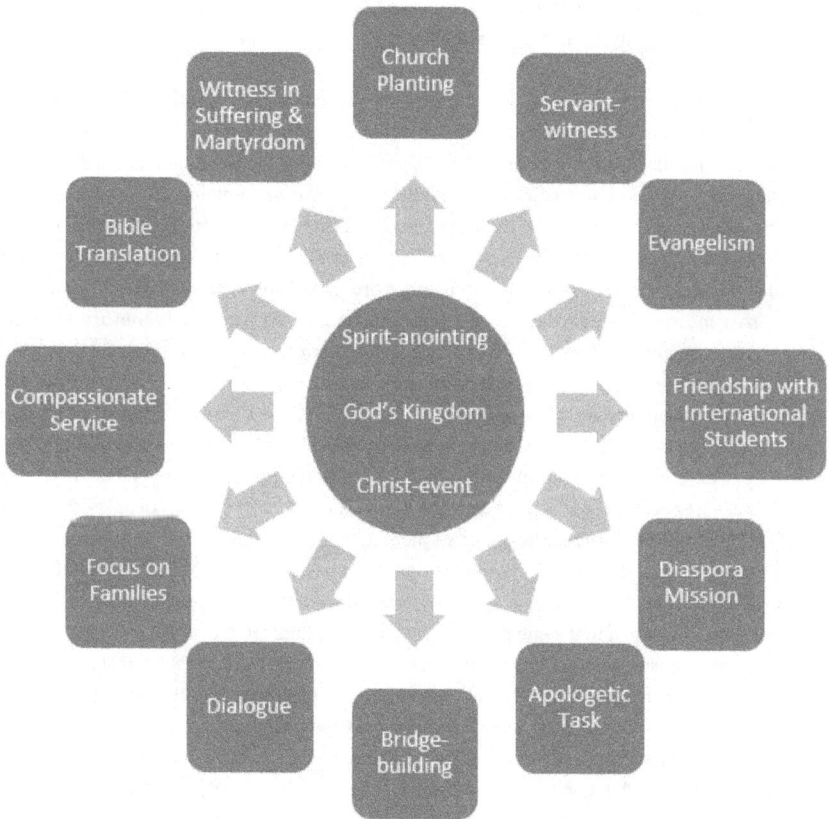

Figure 5: Method of Spirit-Anointed Witness in Holistic Mission

Church Planting

The effective cause of people coming to faith in Jesus Christ and becoming active members of local communities of followers of Jesus is the power of God and of the Holy Spirit. The offer of salvation as liberation from guilt and sin, the offer of hope for existence after death, the offer of a transformed life over impure passions, and the offer of fellowship with people from all walks of life were attractive and powerful convictions and realities that Paul could place in the center of his missionary proclamation. One of the methods suggested by Donald McGavran was the consistent focus on" people groups" or homogeneous units, defined as a section of society in which all the members have some characteristic in common.[168] It is claimed that church planters who enable unbelievers to become Christians without crossing social, linguistic, or class barriers, are much more effective than those

---

[168] Donald A McGavran, *Understanding Church Growth*, 3rd ed., (Grand Rapids: Eerdmans, 1990), 69.

who place these in the way. The basic assumption is that the main barrier to conversion is not religious or theological, but sociological. However, the pragmatic argument of effectiveness clearly is not sufficient to justify its use in missionary work that aims at establishing new communities of followers of Jesus.

Paul's letters provide us both with a paradigm and with a biblical principle for evaluating methods of proclaiming the good news and of establishing Christian communities of followers of Christ. In Paul's first letter to the church in Corinth, he insists on the fundamental significance of the proclamation of Jesus, the crucified and risen Messiah and Savior, not only for one's personal salvation but for all areas of the life of new converts and of the church. Paul's emphasis on the unity of a local congregation in which Jews, proselytes, God-fearers, and Greeks and Romans who have come to faith in Jesus Christ, live, learn, and worship together proceeds from the foundational significance of the missionary message he preached. Since there is one God, the Father from Whom are all things and for Whom we exist, and one Lord, Jesus Christ, through Whom are all things and through Whom we exist (1 Cor. 8:6), the unity of the believers in a local congregation follows.[169] Paul established congregations of followers of Jesus Christ irrespective of their ethnic, cultural, or social identity, insisting on the unity of the local expression of the people of God. The missionary journeys by the apostles resulted in the formation of Churches. Elders were appointed as overseers (Acts 14:23).

In Acts 2:42, Luke described the first Christian Church in which God's people became the Spirit-filled body of Christ. These earliest church members devoted themselves to four major disciplines. The first evidence of the Spirit-renewed church was concentrated study. They devoted themselves to the teachings of the Apostles. True apostolic succession continues wherever a Christian Community continues steadfastly in that same doctrine the Lord communicated through the apostles. The second evidence of a Spirit-renewed church was fellowship. At the core of their structure was *koinonia*, shared things in common. It is a structure built around the fellowship of the Holy Spirit (2 Cor. 13:14). The third evidence of the Spirit-renewed church was spiritual worship. They devoted themselves to the breaking of bread and prayers. The Spirit-filled community was a worshipping community. They regularly broke bread in consistent observance of the Lord's supper (Acts 2:46b). They ate together with great joy and they praised God (Acts 2:46-47). The fourth evidence of a Spirit-renewed church was a committed membership. The record says that the Lord added to their number daily those who were being saved (Acts 2:47). John Stott writes, "He does not save them without adding them to the Church, and He does not add them to the Church without saving them."[170]

Their witness in evangelism was the overflow of their fellowship, their joyful life of praise, and their persistence in the apostolic teaching, in fact, their concern for relationships. They related to the apostles, related to one another, related to God, and related to the Head of the body. This resulted in consistent allegiance to the local assembly, and witness to those outside the Christian community.[171]

[169] Rene Padilla, "The Unity of the Church and the Homogeneous Unit Principle," *International Bulletin of Missionary Research* 6, no 1 (1982), 23-30.
[170] John R W Stott, *Your Mind Matters*, (Downers Grove: InterVarsity Press, 1972), 20.
[171] Del Birkey, *The House Church: A Model of Renewing the Church*, (Scottdale, PA: Herald Press 1988, 1993), 155.

Servant Witness

At the second Lausanne conference held in Manila (1989) the manifesto, quoted by Chris Green in "The Incarnation and Mission," states, "true mission is incarnational, it necessitates entering humbly into other people's worlds, identifying with their social reality, their sorrow and suffering, and their struggles for justice against powers."[172]

John Stott argued at the Lausanne conference held in 1974 that the Johannine text 20:19-23 is the crucial form of the Great Commission. "... Jesus said, 'Peace be with you, as the Father has sent Me, I am sending you,' with that He breathed on them and said, 'Receive the Holy Spirit. If you forgive anyone's sins, their sins are forgiven; if you do not forgive them, they are not forgiven.'" Just as Christ identified with us in becoming a human, we too need to identify with those whom we are trying to reach with the love of God. However, the emphasis in Jesus' words is not identification, rather on the reception of the Holy Spirit and the promise of the Holy Spirit. As Andreas Kostenberger rightly comments, the fact that Jesus shows to His disciples His pierced hands and His side (cf. 20:19-20), as well as His commission to forgive or retain sins, ties the disciples' mission to Jesus' death.[173] Todd Billings explores the implication of Jesus saying "receive the Holy Spirit" as follows: it is not our own incarnation, but the Holy Spirit Who makes Christ present in us and beyond us. In Billings' view, the New Testament model for Mission is not an incarnational one but the much richer theology of servant witness and cross-cultural ministry...in union with Christ by the Spirit.[174]

Jesus asked the early disciples, "come ... Take My yoke upon you and learn from Me, for I am gentle and lowly in heart, and you will find rest for your souls" (Matt. 11:28). Jesus categorically stated, "Even the Son of Man didn't come to be served but to serve and give His life as a ransom for many" (Mark 10:45). A missionary with a servant heart will receive successful entry among people and into other cultures.

Paul often presented himself as an apostle to clarify the authority with which he treated difficult moral matters in his letters. He also considered himself a servant even in those contexts (Rom. 1:1, 1 Cor. 3:5, Phil. 1:1, Titus 1:1). A few principles of servanthood may be traced from a Pauline perspective:[175]

1. The missionary must serve the good of the people and not for his or her own designs (2 Cor. 12:14).
2. He or she must serve even though it is not recognized and appreciated (2 Cor. 12:15).
3. The missionary should serve to edify others and not to make personal claims (2 Cor. 12:16-19).
4. He or she should serve believing that God is conscious of what is being done whether other people are conscious of it or not (2 Cor. 12:19).
5. The missionary must serve although the results are not what he or she had hoped for (2 Cor. 12:20).
6. The missionary must serve with a spirit of humility (2 Cor. 12:21).

---

[172] Chris Green, "The Incarnation and Mission," in D G Peterson (ed), *The Word Became Flesh: Evangelicals and the Incarnation* (Carlisle: Paternoster, 2003), 110-111.
[173] Andreas Kostenberger, The Missions of Jesus and the Disciples According to the Fourth Gospel (Grand Rapids: Eerdmans, 1998), 195.
[174] Todd J Billings, "The Problem with Incarnational Ministry," *Christianity Today*, July-August 2012, 60.
[175] Terry, Smith, and Anderson (eds), 342-343.

Paul was conscious that even though he had taught and led the Corinthians with a Christian Spirit, some of them continued to live carnally, especially in their relationship with one another. New believers in the Two-thirds World often come to faith from a spiritist, or idolatrous background and continue to have many relational problems and immoral habits. Patient teaching and modeling is essential for these to grow in their new nature in Christ. Paul also demonstrated a servant spirit when he humbled himself in order to lift the Corinthians up, as well as helping them sense the depth of his concern for their moral struggle (2 Cor. 11:7, 8, 29). Paul's servant spirit led him to express a daily concern for all the churches he and his missionary team had established.

A missionary was invited by a small group of low-caste people to share with them the message of Christian faith in an Indian village. He sat on the mat in the hut, shared the Gospel, and prayed for them, which resulted in that little group trusting in Jesus Christ, receiving Christ, and receiving Christian baptism. They gathered for prayer and worship. One of the converts told the missionary upon his visit at a later period:

"Do you know why we listened so attentively to your words, it was not just what you told us though the story of Jesus Christ was very wonderful and touched our hearts, it was the fact that you as a rich American were willing to come to our humble homes, sit on the dirt floor, eat our meager food, and make yourselves at home with us, that really convinced us that what you were saying was true and caused us to listen with a whole heart."[176]

Evangelism

The Lausanne covenant affirms that "In the Church's mission of sacrificial service, evangelism is primary" (*Evangelism and Mission*, paragraph 6). The reason is well stated by Peter Wagner who calls the Fourth World, namely: the more than 2,700 million unreached peoples of the World. So, evangelism is to be the heartbeat of the Church. Billy Graham defined evangelism in 1983 as the offering of the whole Christ, by the whole Church, to the whole man, to the whole World. The international Missionary council at Tambaram in 1938 expressed, "Evangelism is the transmission of the Gospel of Christ to the whole world with the purpose of saving individual souls..." There are more definitions of evangelism: Kagava said "evangelism means the conversion of people from worldliness to Christlike Godliness," William Temple said that evangelism is the winning of men to acknowledge Christ as their Savior and King, so that they may give themselves to His service in the fellowship of His Church. The Evanston Assembly in 1954 spoke of Evangelism as the bringing of persons to Christ as Savior and Lord that they may share in His eternal life. John Stott advocates that evangelism is neither to convert people, nor to win them, nor to bring them to Christ, though this is indeed a primary goal of evangelism. Evangelism is to preach the Gospel.[177] He holds this view to prove that evangelism should not be defined in terms of results. For example, "there they evangelized," meaning "they preached the Gospel" (Acts 14:7, cf. Rom.15:20). But, the Spirit-anointed witness of a Christian disciple engages in this act for the transformation of lives, being saved to serve Christ. Paul writes, "brothers, my heart's desire and prayer to God for the Israelites is that they may be saved" (Rom. 10:1). In evangelism or in witness: the purpose, goal, and act are well integrated. The Spirit-guided

---

[176] John T Seamands, *Tell It Well: Communicating the Gospel Across Cultures*, (Kansas City: Beacon Hill Press, 1981), 95.
[177] Stott and Wright, 61.

persuasion found in the evangelistic crusades of the anointed ones throughout history is the result of the conviction that evangelism is not mere announcing the Gospel but enabling a sinner to accept Jesus Christ as Savior and Lord for eternal life. The urgency of winning the lost to Jesus Christ has been a common thread running through all branches of Pentecostalism. Grant McClung says, "Pentecostals have understood an obedience to evangelize as one of the primary steps in obedience in Christian discipleship."[178]

Most people who commit to Christ will do so through the witness of someone within their own culture; Ralph Winter, at the Lausanne International World conference on World Missions, emphasized cultural distance more than geographical distance from Acts 1:8. Evangelism in the Jerusalem and Judea sphere is called E-1 evangelism, involving the same language and culture. This is near-neighbor evangelism. The second sphere Jesus referred to is that of Samaria. The Jew and Samaritan are divided from each other by a frontier consisting of dialectical distinctions and some other very significant cultural differences. This is E-2 evangelism. It involved crossing of language and/or culture. E-3 evangelism involves even greater cultural distance. This is the third sphere of Jesus' statement, "to the uttermost part of the earth." The people who need to be reached in the third sphere live, work, talk, and think in languages and cultural patterns utterly different from those native to the evangelist.[179]All people groups will not be reached unless there are cross-cultural missionaries willing to move into local cultures, learn the language, and act and speak in ways that point to Jesus.

Regardless of the method used to reach people, a passion for souls is the critical factor in personal evangelism. The passing witnessing contact on the street may well be a divine appointment from God. Paul had the inner conviction of the love of Christ that compelled him to share the Gospel (2 Cor. 5:14). Personal evangelism is a fire in the soul. It is the individual Christian's response to Christ's call to take up the cross and follow Him. It is the free, unhindered flow of the Gospel from the life of a Christian to a lost person.[180] If we love people, we cannot withhold the Gospel. It is God's intention for every Christian to witness. Short-term missions began just after World War II with Operation Mobilization and Youth With A Mission. It is a cross-cultural partnership, which is an important part of the Mission of the Church. The one involved in it personally benefits from becoming more aware of his or her own ethnocentrism, of the existence of the World church, and of cross-cultural practice; it may spark a lifelong commitment to missions or cross cultural partnership that leads to vision, giving, and prayer; there may be genuine benefits, for the place and location where short termers go, in the form of service, gifts, resources, or tasks; short termers may encourage and aid long-term missionaries, cross-cultural workers, and the national Church if the project fits into long-term goals.[181]

"Internet-evangelism" is very relevant in the present context of the technological revolution. Matt Rich, who leads Internet Mission, trains part-time volunteers to use the Web for evangelism, with a particular emphasis on sharing in chat rooms and bulletin boards. One of the things he discovered is

[178] Grant McClung, "A Church Growth Perspective on Pentecostal Missions," in Peter C Wagner, *Called and Empowered: Global Mission in Pentecostal Perspective*, (Peabody, MA: Hendrickson Publishers, 1991), 268.
[179] Ralph Winter, "The New Macedonia: A Revolutionary New Era in Mission Begins," in Winter and Hawthorne (eds), 299.
[180] Darrel W Robinson, "The Priority of Personal Evangelism," in Beougher and Reid (eds), 126.
[181] Michael Goheen, Introducing Christian Mission Today: Scripture, History, and Issues, (Downers Grove: IVP Academic, 2014), 433.

that people may feel too inhibited to talk face to face, but they are often happy to talk about their thoughts and feelings online.[182]

"Sign board evangelism" has become significant in sharing the Gospel in these days. The Church I am currently pastoring (I P C Hebron Los Angeles) uses this method ardently. Members, including kids, stand in different places of the city on the first Saturday of every month with signboards, projecting the Gospel message with great passion. "Christ died for our sins," projected in a carwash station in my local area has great impact upon the people who make use of this station. Stickers used in cars with a short Gospel message are a powerful method in witnessing by Christians all over the World.

Friendship with International Students

Each year over 120,000 new international students and scholars begin a four-year sojourn in American Universities and other institutions for higher learning. There are exhilarating opportunities to shape future leaders at universities in America. As caring and committed Christians come across their paths and offer friendships in Him, these future leaders can learn about the greatest friend of all, Jesus Christ. Immersed in a new culture and away from the family, one may feel lonely and anxious about the future. Developing a friendship will enable an international student to feel comfortable in their life in this nation. Accompany them for shopping, locating housing or banking, entertaining them at home, help finding an inexpensive, reliable car, taking them for sightseeing tours to local sights, helping students with transportation to and from the airport, care for developing communication skills, as well as expressing genuine love and compassion will be great motivation to listen to a witness. As relationships form we can find sensitive ways to respectfully present the claims of Christ and help them grow in Christian faith.

InterVarsity, CRU (formerly Campus Crusade), and the Baptist Student Union have already established ministries that have impacted many, providing motivation for the emerging generation. International Students, Inc., an organization which has been reaching out to International students for more than 50 years, understands the vital synergy they share with the local church.[183] Inter Collegiate Prayer Fellowship (ICPF), founded in Kerala, India, makes attempts to reach out to students on college campuses. ICPF impacted Cambodia along with campuses in South East Asia. International student ministry is a unique opportunity for the church. The Higher Education Research Institute (HERI) released a report with findings from UCLA in spring 2005:

- 80% are interested in spirituality
- 76% are searching for meaning/purpose in life
- 74% have discussions about the meaning of life with friends
- 81% attend religious services
- 80% discuss religion or spirituality with friends
- 79% believe in God

---

[182] Matt Rich, "The Internet Mission," in Ron Boehme, *The Fourth Wave: Taking Your Place in the New Era of Missions,* (Seattle, WA: YWAM Publishing, 2011), 159-160.
[183] Pete Briscoe and Todd Hillard, The Surge: Churches Catching the Wave of Christ's Love for the Nations, (Grand Rapids: Zondervan, 2010), 97.

- 69% pray.[184]

Despite these facts, students are not necessarily given opportunities to hear the Gospel. Nevertheless, they do appreciate honest conversation about spiritual matters more than a rehearsed monologue presentation.

Bhaktsingh, a Sikh man, came from Northern India to study Engineering in Canada. A Christian couple reached out to Bhaktsingh in friendship and love. They gave a Bible and encouraged him to meet other Christians. Through their friendship, he accepted Christ. The couple also taught him the scriptures. He went back to India not only as an engineer but as a preacher and evangelist. As a result of his faithful work for Christ, over 700 Churches have been established in India, Pakistan, Sri Lanka, and Nepal.[185]

Diaspora Mission

The United States of America is the largest and most favored destination for migrant masses globally. The US has the largest foreign-born population in the World (in 1990 it was 19.6 million, 8% of the total population and in 2003, it had grown to 33.5 million, 11.7% of the population). The vibrant economy, education, opportunities, and free society make it an attractive proposition for people everywhere to emigrate.[186]

Immigrants in the United States of America have been steadily increasing since 1965 with the Indian Historical Heart Cellar Act. Indians are the fourth largest community following Mexico, China, and Philippines. Large Indian diaspora exist in every state with the five largest among them being California, Texas, New York, New Jersey, and Illinois. According to a survey conducted by the Pew Forum on Religion and Public Life, Hindus account for 0.4 of the total US population (data collected in 2012). Significant concepts such as the law of Karma, re-incarnation, and the practice of yoga have become part of the main stream of American population. It is found in the article "We are all Hindus Now" by Lisa Miller that 24% of the American population believe in the doctrine of re-incarnation, a core concept of Hinduism.[187] This shows the impact of Hinduism in this nation, and many Americans have become devotees of different organizations under the wide umbrella of the Hindu religion which is very inclusive in its nature. There are over 1000 Indian American organizations across the country. Indian Americans have attained high degrees of professionalism and are most prevalent in the fields of science and technology. "Nearly 27% of IT professionals are Indian Americans. 30,000 Indian Americans are practicing in hospitals and over 5,000 Indian American faculty members are teaching in various universities in the nation."[188] They have the highest rate of educational attainment and household income among immigrants in the USA. 48% hold a post-graduate degree at a household income of $100,000 or more. They also tend to have the lowest divorce rate among all religious communities.[189] A message on unity of all faiths to the West delivered by Swami Vivekananda from

[184] Edward Pearson, "Effective Methods for Reaching College Students," in Thomas P Johnston (ed), *Mobilizing a Great Commission Church for Harvest*, (Eugene, OR: Wipf and Stock, 2011), 189.
[185] Tom Philipps and Bob Norsworthy, "The World at Your Door," in Winter and Hawthorne (eds), 742-743.
[186] Sam George, *Understanding the Coconut Generation*, (Niles, IL: Mall Publishing, 2006), 13.
[187] Lisa Miller, "We Are All Hindus Now," *Newsweek*, August 15, 2009.
[188] R Gopakumar, *Indian Diaspora and Giving Patterns of Indian Americans in the USA*, (New Delhi, India: Charities Aid Foundation, India, 2003), 12.
[189] Pew Research Forum, *Asian Americans: A Mosaic of Faiths* http://www.pewforum.org/2012/07/19/Asian-americans-a-mosaic-of-faiths-overview. (Accessed October 13, 2014).

India at the Parliament of the World's Religions held at Chicago in 1893 had tremendous influence on intellectuals and proposed to accord a high place to Jesus Christ as one of the great incarnations of God. He was prepared to admit that man needed to be delivered from the darkness of ignorance, but to speak of men as "miserable sinners" was in his judgement a crime. This demonstrates the subtle nature of Hinduism which attracts people, including the young generation, to become adherents of the old religion.

Hinduism has become the third largest religious group in the World after Christianity and Islam. A majority of Hindus live in India or in South Asia. The influence of Hinduism in modern times in the West has been mostly through the New Age movement, the Hare Krishna movement, and transcendental meditation through Yoga teachings. It is significant to learn about India for a passionate mission. Saji Lukos gathered the statistics for pioneering Mission India:

- 4,635 distinct people groups, spread over a geographic area one-third the size of the USA
- 6,400 castes, each functioning as a separate group due to social barriers
- 1,652 languages, with 22 major languages
- 80% Hindu; 13% Muslim; 2.4% Christians (but less than 1% in North India); 2% Sikh; 1% Buddhist
- 300 million middle class people; 600 million live in poverty; 300 million below the poverty line
- 70% of the Indian population lives in 600,000 rural villages.[190]

There is a growing tension in the churches of the Indian diaspora on topics such as Christian identity and evangelism in the context of cultural pluralism, doctrine and practice, eternal hell and heaven, sin and salvation. Most of our churches are passive or ignorant regarding the challenges. Church as a community of faith and witness needs to become engaged in Spirit-anointed witness to the Indian diaspora with a zealous heart.

Here are different points of contact with Christianity, which deserve attention:

- The Hindus system is basically monistic, recognizing the existence of Spirit alone. Christianity accepts both spiritual and material Worlds.
- In Hinduism, God is impersonal, without attributes. In Christianity, God is a Person, with infinite attributes, with whom man can have relationship.
- In Hinduism, the universe is an illusion. Material World and man are mere emanations of God. The Christian faith contends that the World is real, the arena of decision and eternal destiny. Man is created in the image of God, is fallen indeed through disobedience, but has the capacity for fellowship with God.
- In Hinduism, the basic problem is intellectual – ignorance. In Christianity, it is a moral problem – sin.
- In Hinduism, the purpose of incarnation is to destroy the wicked and protect the righteous. In Christianity, the purpose of Christ's incarnation is to seek and save the lost (Luke 19:10).
- In Hinduism, salvation is a release from the wheel of existence and the bondage of Karma (actions) and is achieved through self-effort. In Christianity, salvation is a deliverance from the guilt and power of sin, and is a gift of God, received by faith in Jesus Christ.

---

[190] Saji Lukos, *Transformed for a Purpose*, (Huntley, IL: Mall Publishing, 2016), 54-55.

Evangelism to the Hindu diaspora in the USA is to be the priority of the Churches in setting an agenda for witness. The message to be shared is that Christ is the fulfillment of the noble aspirations of Hinduism. Jesus said, I am the Way (the *Karma marga* – the method of acting); I am the Truth, (the *Jnana marga* – the method of knowing); I am the Life (the *Bhakti marga* – the object of devotion) (John 14:6).[191] Christ is the answer to the fervent prayer of the Hindu expressed in the Vedas of Hinduism (Religious Scripture):

- "From the untruth lead me to the truth
- "From Darkness lead me to light
- "From death lead me to immortality."

Christian evangelists used this prayer in Hinduism as a point of contact in communicating the Gospel. It is effective and convincing the diaspora. A passionate witness could reach out to those people everywhere with a burden and commitment.

Atul Aghamkar has made a significant study on a contextual missiology for India and the challenge he raised is to be recognized. He writes:

Today, the official census figures indicate that, about one third of India's population lives in urban centers, amounting to about 300 million people, which makes India possibly the largest urbanized nation in the world. If this present trend continues, then within two decades, more than half of India may be found in its cities. In preparing the Church to respond appropriately into the changing context of urban India, the need to inform, educate, equip, and mobilize Christian leaders is to be sensed urgently.[192]

Christian churches in India, especially Pentecostal and Charismatic groups, are rapidly growing despite a surge in persecution. Christian churches are underestimated by the government due to political reasons. "For mid-2010, the Atlas and Global Christianity claims 58.4 Million (4.8% of the total population) and Operation World claims 71 Million (5.8%)."[193] It is not easy to track the growth of Indian Churches, but attempts are made by various organizations. Although Christians are found all over India, certain parts of South India and North East India account for most of the Christian population. Major urban centers in the nation also have a sizable Christian presence (~ 13%) including commercial hubs like Bangalore (6%) and Chennai (5%). Significant growth has also been seen in South Gujarat, Punjab, Chhattisgarh, and Bihar.[194]

Several mega-churches established in the last three decades in India demonstrate the powerful witness of those initiated for the expansion of the Kingdom of God. Calvary Temple in Hyderabad, pastored by Satish Kumar, is reckoned as the largest church in India. It is reported that the church can accommodate 35,000 people and is packed each of its five services every Sunday.[195] Christian

---

[191] Seamands, 165.

[192] Atul Aghamkar, *Mission in the Metropolis: Towards a Contextual Missiology for Urban India*, Sabbatical Research Proposal (Accessed January 1, 2018).

[193] Lausanne Global Analysis, Number of Christians in China and India, 2012
http:// www.lausanne.org/lgc-transfer/number-of-christians-in-china-and-india-2 (Accessed February 28, 2018).

[194] An Indian Christian: Percentage of Christians in India, 2013
http://anindianchristian.blogspot.com/2013/01/percentage-of-christians-in-india.html (Accessed February 28, 2018).

[195] Hazel Torres, "Christians Packing Churches in India as Christianity Sees Surprising Growth Despite Rising Persecution Cases" https://www.christiantoday.com/article/christians-packing-churches-in-india-as-christianity-sees-surprising-growth-despite-rising-persecution-cases/99915.htm

churches are rapidly growing in North India despite the surge in persecution. Numerous house churches have been formed in states like Bihar, Rajasthan, Gujarat, and Maharashtra.

Apologetic Task

We come across people who have several questions in their mind that prevent them from coming to the Christian faith. Many Christians would simply reply, "Well, you have to take it on faith!" or "The Bible says it's true, and that settles it. You have to take God at His Word!" Or some would simply walk away and assume that the person was destined for judgement, unable to see the truth that God has revealed to His true followers. However, the Bible tells we should do whatever it takes to be ready to give a clear and thoughtful response, always "ready to give an answer to everyone who asks you to give the reason for the hope that you have but do this with gentleness and respect" (1 Pet. 3:15). The original Greek word that is translated "answer" in that verse is *apologia*, which means "a speech of defense." It's from this that we get our term apologetics, which is a reasoned defense in our faith. So, all of us who are followers of Christ are to be ready to back up their faith as Spirit-anointed witnesses in the world. Apologetics is the handmaiden to evangelism. It serves, when appropriately applied, the greater purposes of the Gospel and the Christian mission "to go into all the world and make disciples."[196]

We recognize that there are many intellectual obstacles to faith from which several questions emerge. How can anyone claim to have the truth or to know the truth? There are many other holy books. What makes Christians think their book is better than the others? With all the evil and suffering in the World, don't you have to admit that your God is not in control? How could a good and loving God make faith in Jesus the only way to heaven and eternal life? Don't all religions ultimately lead to God?

We do not claim to have all the answers in a convincing manner. But we have more than enough to show that our faith in an omnipotent, omniscient, holy, loving creator God, Who bridged the gap between Himself and humankind in the person of Jesus Christ, is not only reasonable but is, in fact, the most intellectually and existentially coherent option among all others. Christianity is both sensible to the head and satisfying to the heart.[197]

Christians hold that God made Himself known and knowable through the historical figure of Jesus of Nazareth. Jesus Himself claimed to be the Truth (John 14:6) and declared "if you hold to My teaching, you are really My disciple. Then you will know the Truth, and the Truth will set you free" (John 8:31-32). Some critics of Christianity assert, "we all come by different routes and end up in the same place. There are many roads but just one destination." It sounds so all-encompassing and pleasing to the ear. Yet the truth is that all religions are not the same. All religions do not point to God; in fact, some religions do not believe in God.

There is a distinction between an apology and apologetics. An apology refers to a specific defense whereas apologetics refer to the science of making an apology. Apologetics is the branch of Christian theology which seeks to develop principles for making a specific apology. Some have even argued that apologetics is a way of doing theology, as opposed to kerygmatic theology which is concerned with

[196] Norman L Geisler and Chad V Meister (eds), *Reasons for Faith: Making a Case for the Christian Faith,* (Wheaton: Crossway Books, 2007), 18.
[197] Norman L Geisler and Paul K Hoffman (eds), *Why I Am a Christian?,* (Grand Rapids: Baker Books, 2001), 11.

doctrinal exposition. Others have argued that Christian apologetics is done only for the Christian community, but this would make Peter's exhortation meaningless. Peter encouraged Christians to be prepared for an apologetic witness, "But, in your hearts set apart Christ as Lord. Always be prepared to give an answer to everyone who asks you to give reason for the hope that you have. But do this with gentleness and respect" (1 Pet. 3:15-16a). There are numerous New Testament examples of this kind of apologetic activity. The synoptic Gospels, the Gospel of John, and the book of Hebrews, all give evidence of apologetic activity. The apologetic task of Jesus was evident in the argument against the Pharisees on casting out demons (Matt. 12:22-28) and on performing miracles (Luke 7:22-23). Jesus presents five credible witnesses to establish a truth: the witness of John the Baptist, the witness of the Father in Heaven, the witness of the Old Testament, the witness of Moses, and the witness of His works (John 5:31-39). The writer of Hebrews presents the Son as superior to Angels (1:2-4). Paul defends himself before the mob in Jerusalem (Acts 26:2).

The love of Jesus Christ is the answer to the skeptics in the World. Josh McDowell wanted to be happy and to find meaning for his life as a teenager, reflecting on the words of Thomas Aquinas, "there is within every soul a thirst for happiness and meaning." He wanted the answers to three questions: "Who am I? Why am I here? Where am I going?" He estimated that 90 percent of people age forty and younger cannot answer those questions. After a long intellectual struggle in life, he confessed his sins and opened the door of his life to Christ. Josh writes, "I placed my trust in Jesus as Savior and Lord; the love of God inundated my life. He took my hatred for my father and turned it upside down. Five months after becoming a Christian, I found myself looking my Dad right in the eye and saying, 'Dad, I love you.' I didn't want to love that man, but I did. God's love had changed my heart."[198]

Christian commitment is a personal affirmation. No one is born a Christian. Ravi Zacharias writes in "Why I Believe Jesus Christ is the Ultimate Source for Meaning,"

I made that commitment at the age of seventeen. While the moment of my commitment was based on a hunger to know God, the years that have followed have taken me through an intellectual journey. That journey culminated in the conclusion that in Jesus I find not only every hunger of the heart met but also every pursuit of the mind.[199]

Nabeel Qureshi was raised in a Muslim American family before converting to Christianity. His grandparents were Muslim missionaries in Indonesia. Qureshi was a medical doctor as well as holding degrees in theology and philosophy, academic credentials that earned him respect. He was well versed in the faith in which he was raised. The transformation happened after a fellow college student sparked his interest in Christianity, which paved the way for him to work with Ravi Zacharias in Christian Apologetics. Nabeel said that for years as a young man, he labored and struggled to gain righteousness before God only to find out that righteousness was to be found in the cross through Jesus Christ. That was a message in his best-selling book, *Seeking Allah, Finding Jesus*. Though he died at the age of 34 battling stomach cancer, he was passionately evangelistic. He desired to cover the globe with the good news: God's forgiveness is available to all.

The field of apologetics deals with the hard questions posed to the Christian faith. Each of us has a worldview whether we recognize it or not. A worldview basically offers answers to four necessary

[198] Josh McDowell, "Afterword," in Geisler and Hoffman (eds), 284-288.
[199] Ravi Zacharias, "Why I Believe Jesus Christ is the Ultimate Source for Meaning," in Geisler and Hoffman (eds), 268.

questions: origin, meaning, morality, and destiny. Christian apologetics is the discipline of answering people's specific questions and making the truth claims clear. We aim to engage people in meaningful interactions with gentleness and respect, bearing in mind that behind every question is a questioner.[200] Instead of condemning others for their logical inferences and reasonable questions, we need to be persistent with passion for proving that Christ is the answer. Ravi Zacharias sharply asserts that evangelism without apologetics is like setting down your weapons in the heat of a battle.[201] Church in the post-modern age needs to equip well with the method of apologetics. Jesus Christ and the Apostles were apologetic witnesses. Patrick Zukeran in his article "The Apologetics of Jesus," writes, "Christian apologetics use reason and evidence to present a convincing case for Christianity, challenge unbelief, expose errors, and defend the message of the Gospel."[202]

Bridge-Building

Bridge-building is to relate meaningfully to people of a very different culture and religion, to attain mutual understanding, to secure more than superficial change. There is risk of being misunderstood when one becomes involved with this method of bridge-building. The Serampore Trio (Carey, Marshman, and Ward) were misunderstood because of their efforts to understand the culture and religion of India almost two hundred years ago. But they could adapt the presentation of the Gospel most effectively. Charles Kraft believed that "at least half of the so-called heresies identified by the Church councils of the early centuries were not really heresies at all, rather, were legitimate attempts to contextualize the Gospel for pagan people of the time."[203] It is ironic that the Gospel itself can be lost in the effort to accommodate it to other cultures and religions. That is highly questionable. Heresy could be the right name to some, yet, a number of teachings may have been attempts to bridge the gap with people of other cultures.

When we attend to the point of contact with adherents of other religions, we become faithful to our missionary calling. The first point of contact in communicating the Gospel is our attitude and disposition. Our approach will make the Gospel either attractive or unattractive. Our Christ-like communication demonstrating love, humility, openness, empathy, kindness, gentleness, genuine interest in people – their needs, dreams, life situations – revolutionize our witness in a society. Witnessing to the Gospel will mean relevance on the one hand, and challenge on the other. The Gospel answers the deep longings of the heart and challenges the way they are understood.

Theories have abounded in man's search to build natural bridges from the Gospel to non-Christian religions. To think, however, of all religions as alike, interrelated, and originating from the same source and leading to the same conclusions and destiny is a serious mistake. George Peters writes in "Missions in a Religiously Pluralistic World,"

the revelational concept of God as the Father of Jesus Christ as revealed in the Trinity, the creation of the world with its history and purpose, and the biblical doctrine of humanity as created in the image

---

[200] Ravi Zacharias, "Why this Muslim-turned-Christian speaker resonated with so many before his death at 34" https://www.washingtonpost.com/amphtml/news/acts-of-faith/wp/2017/09/17/why-this-muslim-turned-christian-speaker-resonated-with-so-many-before-his-death-at-34 (Accessed October 05,2017).

[201] Pearson, in Johnston (ed), 199.

[202] Patrick Zukeran, "The Apologetics of Jesus," https://bible.org/article/apologetics-jesus, Published September 25, 2009 (Accessed December 16, 2017).

[203] Charles H Kraft, Christianity in Culture: A Study in Dynamic, Biblical Theologizing in Cross-Cultural Perspective, (Maryknoll, NY: Orbis Books, 1979), 287.

of God, fallen into sin, and redemption in Christ, simply cannot be fitted into the ethnic religions of the world...There is a total otherness in revelational Christianity "rightly so-called" and in the Gospel of the Lord Jesus Christ. It simply is incomparable.[204]

Dialogue

The concept of dialogue with people of other faiths has been the ecumenical fashion for at least the last three decades. Here is the question: "Is the evangelical's negative reaction justified scripturally?" The National Evangelical Anglican Congress at Keele in 1967 (Paragraph 83) defined, "Dialogue is a conversation in which each party is serious in his approach both to the subject and to the other person, and desires to listen and learn as well as to speak and instruct." [205] It is important to note that God Himself entered into dialogue with Adam in the Garden of Eden. It is also found in the dialogical approach with Job, "Gird up your loins like a man, I will question you, and you shall declare to Me" (Job 38:3, 40:7). It was true with Jesus, Who was sitting among the teachers, listening and asking questions (Luke 2:46). He was constantly asking questions and provoked counter questions in His ministry on earth (with Nicodemus, the Samaritan woman, and the crowds on occasions). The Apostle Paul used the method in his ministry. He argued from the scriptures, explaining and proving that it was necessary for the Christ to suffer and rise from the dead, saying, "this Jesus Whom I proclaim to you, is the Christ." Luke adds: "some of them were persuaded" (Acts 17:1-4). Here five words are brought together – arguing, explaining, proving, proclaiming, and persuading – which suggest that Paul was comfortable with dialogue as a method in mission (cf. 17:17, 18:4, 19:8-10, 20:7, 24:25).

Dialogue is a form of evangelism which is often effective among intellectuals. In his book *Missions and Unity*, Norman E Thomas includes Paul D Devanandan of the Church of South India who presented the key note address, "Called to Witness," in the WCC's third assembly (New Delhi, 1961). Devanandan declared that "the witness of the Church begins with the congregation as the 'community of the New Age,' but it also must be a witness in a world of other faiths." He challenged Christians "so to engage in serious conversation with persons of other faiths that they would become instruments of interpretation of the Gospel."[206] The Upsala conference in 1968 declared:

a Christian's dialogue with another implies neither a denial of the uniqueness of Christ nor any loss of his own commitment to Christ. The genuinely Christian approach to others is to be human, personal, relevant, and humble. In dialogue we share our common humanity, its dignity and fallenness, and express our common concern for that humanity. It may result in common service to meet human needs.[207]

We live side by side with people of other religious faiths, and this requires ongoing conversation. "Our western sense of superiority of the past often has led to a stance of confrontational monologue that has hindered communication. It is essential that our posture be one of humility and vulnerability,

[204] George Peters, "Missions in a Religiously Pluralistic World," in Roy B Zuk (ed), *Vital Missions Issues: Examining Challenges and Changes in World Evangelism*, (Grand Rapids: Kregel Resources, 1998), 47.
[205] Stott and Wright, 99.
[206] Paul D Devanandan, "Called to Witness," in Norman E Thomas, *Missions and Unity: Lessons from History, 1792-2010*, (Eugene, OR: Cascade Books, 2010), 246.
[207] Vinay Samuel and Albrecht Hauser, Proclaiming Christ in Christ's Way: Studies in Integral Mission: Essays Presented to Walter Arnold on the Occasion of His 60th Birthday, (Eugene, OR: Wipf and Stock 2007), 167.

and a listening ear will be important to repair perceptions of the past."[208] Dialogue is also a recognized and familiar approach in our World, and so a contextualized witness will require that we employ methods that are broadly shared. Moreover, the threats to our global community are very real. While we affirm that true human unity can be found only in Jesus Christ, there is a place to seek proximate justice and peace based on common grace. Such efforts certainly will require mutual dialogue among those of different faiths. Dialogue is an expression of our love for others. John Stott writes,

Dialogue is a token of genuine Christian love, because it indicates our steadfast resolve to rid our minds of prejudices and caricatures which we may entertain about other people; to struggle to listen through their ears and look through their eyes so as to grasp what prevents them from hearing the Gospel and seeing Christ; to sympathize with them in all their doubts, fears, and hang-ups.[209]

Hesselgrave raises a very relevant issue in the context of Christian witness in a religiously pluralistic World, "the question for evangelicals is not shall we engage in dialogue? But in what kinds of dialogue should we engage?"[210] True Christian dialogue will be built on a Trinitarian foundation. We dialogue on the basis of God's creation where Adam is the first man from whom all others were born (Acts 17: 26). So, we share common concerns with our neighbors of different faiths living in a common World.

The shared task of building a culture and society should mean a constant dialogue among different religious traditions that seek a way to find peace and public justice to live together. This is not to discount religious difference – precisely the opposite. What is needed is a committed or principled pluralism that takes seriously the various religious commitments and how they shape the public square. Here, witness and dialogue are held firmly together.[211]

We enter dialogue with different faith commitments and our fundamental identity is as witnesses of Jesus Christ. John Hick distinguishes between confessional dialogue and truth-seeking dialogue. Confessional dialogue is a dialogue on the basis of a commitment to the truth of one's faith. Hick rejects this, asserting for him, "this kind of dialogue will end either in conversion or in a hardening of differences."[212] Hick calls for a shift to truth-seeking dialogue, in which adherents of the faiths engage in dialogue for a mutually enriched understanding of the Transcendent Being. However, such a contrast is false. One cannot separate "confession" from "truth seeking." A confession of faith will always be the starting point for seeking more understanding of the truth.

Finally, dialogue will be on the basis of the Holy Spirit. It is the Spirit's work to convince the World of sin, righteousness, and judgement (John 16:7-11). Conversion is not our work, rather, that of the Holy Spirit. Our witness to Christ amid dialogue may lead to the conversion of our neighbor, and it may be the case that the Spirit will convert us more fully to the Gospel (cf. Acts 10).

Stephen Bevans and Roger Schroeder believe that, in coming decades the Church's promotion of Interreligious dialogue may be one of its greatest missionary services in a World in which confrontation and violence is on the increase. "It will be an engaged dialogue of persons who witness

[208] Goheen, 365.
[209] Stott and Wright, 81.
[210] David Hesselgrave, "Interreligious Dialogue – Biblical and Contemporary Perspectives," in Theology and Mission: Papers and Responses Prepared for the Consultation on Theology and Mission, Trinity Evangelical Divinity School, School of World Mission and Evangelism, March 22-25, 1976 (Grand Rapids: Baker Books, 1978), 229.
[211] Goheen, 366.
[212] John Hick, God has Many Names, (Philadelphia: Westminister Press, 1982), 121.

to truth as they understand and experience it. It will be a prophetic dialogue demanding honesty, conviction, courage, and faith."[213]

Stanley E Jones, an American Methodist minister in India 1907-1973, initially working among the low castes realized that he must turn to high caste intellectuals. The strain was too over-whelming and he went through mental breakdown more than once. However, he underwent a deep spiritual experience when great peace settled into his heart, and experienced abundant life. Christ was the focal point of Jones's evangelism, not Christianity. He was convinced that if the educated Indians had the opportunity to see Christ without all his western garb, they would gladly receive him. In presenting Christ to the non-Christians of India, Jones sought to use methods that were a natural part of Indian society. His Round Table Conference and his Christian Ashrams were examples of this. The Round Table Conferences began after he had been invited to a Hindu home to join other intellectuals in philosophical discussions as they all sat in a circle on the floor. With that example, Jones began doing the same thing, inviting Christians as well as adherents of Hinduism, Jainism, and Islam. These discussions, though intellectually oriented, became an avenue for evangelism. He writes, "There was not a single situation that I can remember where before the close of the Round Table Conference Christ was not in moral and spiritual command of the situation."[214] By 1940 there were two dozen Christian ashrams located throughout India. Fundamentalists in Christianity criticized him for his method of making it more appealing to other religious groups and viewed it as compromising Christianity. Though he was often criticized by both the liberals and conservatives, he had a conviction that not institutional Christianity, but Christ must be paramount.

Sadhu Sundar Singh, a pioneer native missionary evangelist in India, used to tell a story illustrating the importance of presenting the Gospel in culturally acceptable terms:

A high caste Hindu had fainted one day from the summer heat while sitting on a train in the railway station. A train employee ran to a water faucet, filled a cup with water and brought it to the man in an attempt to revive him. But in spite of his condition the Hindu refused. He would rather die than accept water in the cup of someone from another caste. Then a high caste passenger filled it with water and offered to the victim who immediately accepted the water with gratitude. Sundar Singh would say to his hearers, "this is what I have been trying to say to the missionaries from abroad. You have been offering the water of life to the people of India in a foreign cup, and we have been slow to receive it. If you offer it in our own cup – in an indigenous form – then we are much more likely to accept it."[215]

Focus on Families

Family is the oldest institution founded by God. The Lord God made a woman from the rib He had taken out of the man and she was brought before him (Gen. 2:22). Man recognized her and expressed intimacy because of the profound mystery in this divine act. For this reason, a man will leave his father and mother and be united to his wife, and they will become one flesh (2:24). The male and female are to be united in marriage according to the design of God. Jesus Christ emphasized the original intention

---

[213] Stephen Bevans and Roger Schroeder, in Thomas, *Missions and Unity*, 262.
[214] Stanley E Jones, in Ruth A Tucker, "Jerusalem to Irian Jaya," in *A Biographical History of Christian Missions*, (Grand Rapids: Baker House, 1983), 332.
[215] K P Yohannan, *Revolution in World Missions*, (Carrollton, TX: GFA Books, 2001), 144.

of God that a man has only one wife and the marriage relationship should supersede the parental relationship (Matt. 19:4-6). Glenn T Stanton writes, "Jesus Christ is telling us that the union of husband and wife is the only sexual union honored and permitted by God. All others – heterosexual, homosexual, or otherwise – are contrary to God's will and design."[216] This ideal family life is a strong foundation in Christianity where values are upheld. It is a complimentary relationship in which partners realize that they exist for each other. It is an ever-growing relationship for revealing the glory of God. It is a covenantal relationship which brings stability in life. Christian family is a corrective force, where family values are everywhere being deteriorated.

In Paul's missionary work, the *oikos*, that is "the private house" and the family of the house owner, was the missionary work, possibly the foundational center of a local church, even the location of the assembly for worship. The house or family was the most fundamental social reality in the ancient World. The house included not only husband and wife, parents and children, but other dependents, relatives and friends, as well as slaves. Paul's missionary work led to the conversion not only of individuals, but sometimes of entire houses, that is, of households or families. In Philippi, the household of Lydia, the purple merchant and the household of the prison official became Christians (Acts 16:14-15, 32-34). In Corinth, the household of Crispus, the Synagogue ruler and the household of Stephanas became believers in Jesus Christ (Acts 18:8, 1 Cor. 1:16, 16:15).[217]

We come across the tragic break-up in family life all over the World. It is a demonic strategy to bring tension in a family for no silly matters. Divorce has become a fashion in the west. Churches don't teach that God hates divorce (Mal. 2:16) and/or the principle that what God has joined together let man not separate (Matt. 19:6). According to a report on Gay marriage around the World navigated by Pew Research Religion and Public Life project, several countries allow gay marriage and in some countries, it is legalized in some jurisdictions. Netherlands (2000), Belgium (2003), Spain (2005), South Africa (2006), Norway (2009), Sweden (2009), Portugal (2010), Iceland (2010), Argentina (2010), Denmark (2012), Uruguay (2013), New Zealand (2013), England/Wales (2013), Brazil (2013), France (2013), Scotland (2014), and the USA (2016).

Many influential figures in the mass-media and technology are proud of becoming gay and propagate this depraved practice in the community. It is unfortunate to note that Episcopal Church leadership in the West is silent at this time on this topic and a few priests are in support of this demonic cultural practice. The sanctity of marriage is lost. "Marry to get divorced, and divorce to get married" has become a popular saying in this perverted generation. Billy Graham wrote, "Christian family life is a holy bond because it permits two people to help each other to work out their spiritual destinies."[218]

The role of Christian Churches is to be obedient to the revelation of God in presenting the Gospel of Christ which demands transformation. Jesus Christ is our example in not condemning sinners, rather extending grace with a clear warning, "go now and leave your life of sin" (John 8:11). The power of the Gospel and its transformation is very evident in any lifestyle tainted by sin. The Church has

---

[216] Glen T Stanton, "Being Authentically Christian on the LGBT issue," in Sean McDowell, *A New Kind of Apologist: Adopting Fresh Strategies, Addressing the Latest Issues, Engaging the Culture,* (Eugene, OR: Harvest House Publishers, 2016), 214.
[217] Eckhard J Schanbel, *Paul the Missionary: Realities, Strategies, and Methods,* (Downers Grove: IVP Academic, 2008), 303-304.
[218] Billy Graham, *The Inspirational Writings,* (New York: Inspirational Press, 1995), 152.

good news in every context of life which brings love, hope, and destiny. Millard J Erickson writes of the Gospel, "it is the Church's sacred trust today. In an age in which most ideas and systems of thought, as well as techniques and commodities, are of a throwaway variety, the church has an infallible and enduring resource – a message which is the only means of salvation."[219] Healthy Christian families constitute a healthy Church which strengthens values in a community where God's glory is revealed.

The foundation for this method of witness is found in Jesus Christ. Jesus healed the demon possessed man in the region of the Gerasenes, which resulted in his request to follow Jesus. Instead of allowing him to join the group He said, "go home to your family and tell them how much the Lord has done for you and how He has had mercy on you" (Mark 5:18-20). The Apostle Paul mainly focused on families and households in mission. He assumed that once the Gospel took root in a home and among family members it would eventually make an impact on the entire community (Gal. 6:10); it refers to more than one set of parents with their children. This includes everyone living together and related to one another, plus friends, servants, even neighbors and guests in their homes.[220] Extended families living together are common in many parts of the World. Paul made his first converts in the environment of the home nearly everywhere he preached. Those baptized were baptized together and shared the Holy Communion together. The church is a family of God and the transforming life of the Kingdom is reflected in it.

Compassionate Service

The Bible teaches that God is conscious of and concerned for all human needs – the physical as well as the spiritual. We need to recognize that meeting the physical and emotional needs of the people must ultimately be a means to an end, namely meeting the spiritual needs of humanity around the World. Jesus Himself was the perfect model and example of this approach to mission in His earthly ministry. Jesus was compassionate toward people who were living with chaotic situations. Christians remained in Alexandria during the bubonic plague of AD 256 to care for the sick and dying while the rest of the population fled. The terms "hospital" and "hospice" derive from hospitality, given the long-established practice from early Centuries of the Church.[221]

Bob Pierce, the founder of Samaritan's Purse often shared the prayer that was the driving force behind his compassionate service: "Let my heart be broken by the things that break the heart of God." Their mission is to work through local Churches and evangelical missions to meet emergency needs so that the Gospel can be shared continually on the various fields. Franklin Graham, President of this organization writes,

It is a ministry of compassion and concern, a ministry to match the gifts of God's people with the recognized needs of those across the world regardless of race or creed. God is using the unique opportunities of meeting people's physical needs to open the doors to their hearts and minister to their spiritual lives. This is just another in the long string of creative methods that the Lord has brought about for sharing the good news of the Gospel.[222]

---

[219] Erickson, 1065.
[220] Roger S Greenway, *Go and Make Disciples: An Introduction to Christian Missions:* (Phillipsburg, NJ: P&R Publishing, 1999), 63.
[221] David Lundy, *Borderless Church: Shaping the Church for the 21st Century,* (Bletchley, UK: Authentic Media, 2005), 57.
[222] Franklin Graham, in Rainer (ed), 167.

Jesus' statement in John 14:12 was not primarily referring to the performing of miracles, rather, He was talking about the methods, the tools, and the resources that He was going to provide for His servants through the Holy Spirit as they faithfully carried the Gospel to everyone.

Mother Teresa, a missionary to India who was awarded the Nobel Peace Prize in 1979 is highly regarded for her selfless service. Born Agnes Bojaxhiu in Albania in 1910, the youngest of three children, she lived in modest comfort until her father died. Despite poverty, her mother was known in the community for helping others. Her mother's devout faith and devotion also had a profound influence on young Agnes who decided to be a missionary in India. She sailed to Bengal in 1929 and after two years of training as a novice, she took her vows to become a Loreto Sister, serving as a teacher specializing in Geography, a position she held for several years until she was named headmistress.

This Loreto Sister's call to minister to the poorest of the poor did not come from a sense of pity for the sick and homeless in Calcutta. She told her spiritual director, Father Julien Henry, "I was travelling to Darjeeling (for my annual retreat), when I heard the voice of God." Father Henry then asked her how she had heard His voice above the noise of a rattling train and she had replied with a smile: "I was sure it was God's voice. I was certain that He was calling me. The message was clear: I must leave the convent to help the poor by living among them. This was a command, something to be done, something definite. I knew where I had to be. But I didn't know how to get there."[223]

Mother Teresa with her unique brand of faith and compassion was able to alleviate loneliness, hunger, and destitution by reaching out through a worldwide mission that provided a presence in 123 countries by the time she died in 1997. She cared for millions of abandoned, homeless, and dying destitute, irrespective of their religion, caste, faith, or denomination.[224] Mother Theresa's anointed witness for compassionate service is highly recognized, though a Catholic nun. She was consistent and courageous to share the Gospel of love even before a large audience. The love of Jesus Christ was the theme for her witness in words and action.

Ida Scudder received the call for medical mission in India while she made a short trip from the USA to care for her mother in sickness. She heard a knock at the door in the night, of three different men – a Brahmin, another high caste Hindu, and a Muslim – pleading for her to assist in difficult childbirths, refusing the assistance of her physician-father because custom prohibited such contact. She spent much of the time in anguish and prayer to seek guidance. She woke up in the morning and heard of the deaths of those three young girls who hadn't received medical assistance. That was the first time she ever met with God and heard God was calling her for this work. She went back to study medicine in the USA in 1895, returned with a compassionate heart, and founded a hospital which has become Vellore Medical College in Tamilnadu. Her broad vision resulted in building a nursing school for women which had impact all over the World. In addition to her medical courses, Scudder taught four-year Bible courses on the Apostle Paul and Pauline epistles.[225] Ida Scudder, the missionary doctor, will be remembered for her compassionate service in Christian holistic mission.

[223] Anne Sebba, *Mother Teresa: Beyond the Image,* (New York: Doubleday, 1998), 46.
[224] Navin Chawla, "Conscience-keeper of her century: Mother Theresa dedicated her life to alleviating hunger and destitution," http://www.dailymail.co.uk/indiahome/indianews/article-2401120/Mother-Theresa-dedicated-life-alleviating-loneliness-hunger-destitution.html, Published August 2013 (Accessed October 29, 2017).
[225] Tucker, 368-370.

Compassionate service includes the involvement of churches and organizations for relief work and development: Natural disasters like earthquake, hurricane, flooding, wildfire, and ethnic violence result in millions of homeless refugees fleeing from numerous locations to other locations in the World which become arenas for holistic mission. Millions of homeless street children and people infected with AIDS seek a demonstration of love and care everywhere. Poverty is a social phenomenon with many expressions such as homelessness, hunger, unemployment, debt, bad credit, and poor education. We need to address the Gospel primarily and care for the poor intentionally.[226]

Bible Translation

The Bible is the most translated book in the World. This was done with a clear perspective in Mission that the message of the Lord may spread rapidly and be honored everywhere (2 Thess. 3:1). The history of Bible translations in India begins with the arrival of Bartholomew Ziegenbalg (German missionary) at the Danish settlement of Tranquebar in 1706. He had a remarkable gift for languages and had completed the translations of the New Testament within five years of his arrival in Tamil land. It was published in 1714, and by 1719, the year of his death, he had finished the Old Testament up to the book of Ruth. The remaining work was completed by another German missionary, Benjamin Schultz, and published in Tranquebar in 1728. Philip Fabricius, also a German, spent 24 years on the translation of the Bible which was published in 1777.[227] The educational aspect of the witness in Mission was the central focus of William Carey and the team (Serampore Trio) in India from 1793. A large printing establishment was set up and Carey spent hours every day in Bible translation. He translated the whole Bible in Bengali, Sanskrit, and Marathi; helped in other whole Bible translations; and translated the New Testament and portions of Scripture into many more languages and dialects.[228]

In 1917, a missionary named William Cameron Townsend went to Guatemala to sell Spanish Bibles. He was shocked when many people couldn't understand because they spoke Cakchiquel, a language without a Bible. He started a linguistics school that trained people to do the translation. The work continued to grow and in 1942, Cam officially founded Wycliffe Bible Translations: the first translation completed in 1951, all the way to the 500th translation completed in 2000. Wycliffe adopted a new challenge – a goal – Vision-2025: a Bible translation project started in every language.[229]

In 2011, the Bible or parts of the Bible were available in 2,527 of the World's 6,500 languages including the entire Bible in 469 languages, and the New Testament in 1,231 languages, according to the United Bible Societies. The United Bible Societies is a federation of 145 national groups that do much of the translation today and is part of the mission history.[230] Christians answer a call of God by

---

[226] Kyle Faircloth, "Mission to Buddhists," in Ashford (ed), 108.
[227] Bible Society of India, *History of Translations: The First Bible to be Translated in India* www.bsind.org/tamil_bible_translations.html (Accessed December 12, 2017).
[228] Tucker, 127.
[229] Wycliffe, "The History of Wycliffe," https://www.wycliffe.org/about (Accessed December 16, 2017).
[230] Global Ministries: The United Methodist Church, "Bible Translation as Mission," http://www.umcmission.org/Learn-About-Us/News-and-Stories/2011/May/Bible-Translation-as-Mission, (Accessed September 15, 2017).

taking the task seriously to meet the challenge from the World to each have a Bible in their own language, and even various versions available in many languages. This could be accomplished with the co-operation of the Churches in promoting committed people and supporting them financially for long years to achieve the given task.

Witness in Suffering and Martyrdom

God entered into history by sending His Son as a Servant to endure suffering and sacrifice. Christianity grew in the context of suffering from the first Century. The place we are called to witness is often a hostile World. The children of God have become partakers of the divine nature (2 Pet. 1:4). Suffering is integral in Christian discipleship. It begins when one leaves all bindings of the World for the priorities set by the Master. The testimony of Stephen resulted in suffering and martyrdom (Acts chapter 7). The early saints had a realistic approach towards suffering. When the apostles were flogged and ordered not to speak in the name of Jesus, they left the Sanhedrin rejoicing because they had been counted worthy of suffering disgrace for Jesus Christ (Acts 5:40-41).

Sadhu Sundar Singh, an itinerant evangelist who was a convert from the Sikh religion, witnessed of Christ in India, Tibet, and Nepal, suffered much for the cause of Christ, including prison, beatings, and being thrown in a grave with rotting bodies. He proclaimed, "formerly the cross was a symbol of disgrace and death, but now it denotes victory and life. Those who bear the cross know from experience that the cross bears them and takes them safely to their destiny."[231]

Martyrdom is the function God gives to some of His elect to literally die for the sake of Christ and His Gospel. From what the Scriptures intimate, it is apparent that there is a fixed number of God's children who have been predestined by God for this supreme sacrifice.[232] Many Christians around the World are persecuted for the sake of the Gospel. "It is reported that the persecution hit a record high in 2016-17. The primary cause of Muslim extremism, now has a rival: ethnic nationalism. Asia increasingly merits concern alongside the Middle East."[233]

Graham Staines, a missionary at Manoharpur village, Odisha, India, burned alive with two children, Philip and Timothy on 22 January 1999, was one of the instances of persecution. He was working among tribal leprosy patients for nearly 30 years with great passion for the sake of the Gospel. The Hindu religious fanatics poured petrol on their car and set it on fire. His wife Gladys, who continued to stay there with her daughter Esther responded to the media, "I have forgiven the killers and have no bitterness because forgiveness brings healing and our land needs healing from hatred and violence."[234] Missionary existence is life in Christ, and life in Christ is a call to be faithful unto death. David Bosch is right in observing that the Missionary is called to die. It is a profound and deep mystery that God has woven into the fabric of redemption.[235]

---

[231] Sadhu Sundar Singh, *Reality and Religion: Meditations on God, Man, and Nature*, (Madras: Christian Literature Service, 1974), 36.
[232] Josef Tson, "Suffering and Martyrdom: God's Strategy in the World," in Winter and Hawthorne (eds), 181-182.
[233] Perry Chiaramonte, "Christians the Most Persecuted Group in the World," *Fox News*, Published January 06, 2017.
[234] Aakash Joshi, "Remembering Graham Staines, 17 Years After His Murder," *The Quint*, Published January 2017, https://www.thequint.com/news/india/remembering-graham-staines-17-years-after-his-murder. (Accessed December 12, 2017).
[235] Bosch, in Sunquist, 408-409.

Jesus' words, "unless a kernel of wheat falls to the ground and dies, it remains only a seed. If it dies, it produces many seeds" (John 12:24), refer not only to the convert but also to the missionaries. Christian witness cannot be done in comfort zones. The orientation is needed that a missionary is called to follow the path of Jesus. We cannot expect anything other than what Jesus encountered in the World.

Summary

The message of Christian witness is unique. God initiated the reconciliatory act in Christ because of His love towards humanity. The walls of hostility are broken down and true relationship is restored by the atonement of Jesus Christ. The ministry of reconciliation is entrusted to us which is vertical and horizontal. The message of reconciliation is relevant in the context where people are segregated socially, religiously, and linguistically all over the World. Reconciliation with God is foundational for salvation and peaceful co-existence in the present life. The practitioners in Christian mission are challenged to find the right method in a changing World. Several methods are included in these chapters which are already employed by missionaries. The Spirit-anointed witness in holistic Christian mission will be effective only when ministry is guided by the text and motivated by the context with a realistic approach.

CHAPTER 6
SCOPE AND GOAL OF SPIRIT-ANOINTED WITNESS

Introduction

The scope is defined as the extent of the area or subject matter that something deals with or to which it is relevant. Christian Mission in the past was carried out from the west to other parts of the World. There have been attempts to send missionaries from one end to the other to fulfill the Great Commission. Since diaspora missiology in relational paradigm is in progress, the scope is clearly articulated that every Christian disciple becomes a witness everywhere. A goal is an idea of the desired result that a person or a group of people envisions, plans, and commits to achieve. Goals increase persistence, greater effort, and task-relevant knowledge and strategies. Christian witness is with the ultimate goal that everyone beholds the glory of God.

Dynamic of Anointed Witness: Spirit-Anointing

The day of Pentecost marked the new beginning. It is widely accepted that the prophecy in Joel 2:28 was fulfilled on that day with missional significance. Hollenweger writes, "The traditional churches are still stuck between Easter and Pentecost."[236] Although they know that Jesus died and rose again, they lack the Pentecostal power which fell on the disciples when they were behind closed doors, drove them out, and made them into courageous witnesses to the Gospel. The Holy Spirit plays a major role in God's program and in Luke – Acts. "There are 16 direct references of the Holy Spirit in Luke's Gospel and at least 57 references in Acts of the Apostles, as the driving force in energizing and guiding events."[237] A majority of Pentecostals believe that baptism in the Holy Spirit is subsequent to conversion experience and water baptism. It is witnessed by the initial sign of speaking with other tongues as the Spirit gives utterance. Donald Gee, Harod Horton, Karel Hoekendijk, Vincent Synan, and Hollenweger are notable among those who defend this position. Jean Stone summed up the result

---

[236] W J Hollenweger, *The Pentecostals: The Charismatic Movement in the Churches*, (Minneapolis: Augsburg Publishing, 1972), 330.
[237] Bock and Kostenberger, 211.

of the baptism of the Spirit in the following way, "it brought a deeper understanding of the love of God, a desire to read the Bible; experience of the Baptism of the Spirit enabled the one to believe in the infallibility of the Scripture, it brought a deeper recognition of sin, power to testify, and power to pray for the sick."[238]

Donald W Dayton writes that "Pentecost" of the New Testament was the "early rain," the outpouring of the Spirit that accompanied "the planting." And modern "Pentecostalism" is the "latter rain" in the special outpouring of the Spirit that restores the gifts in the last days as part of the preparation for "the harvest," the return of Christ in glory.[239] D Martyn Lloyd-Jones, in *Baptism and Gifts of the Spirit*, writes, "the one great function of the baptism with the Holy Spirit is something that applies only to power, power to witness."[240]

Classical Pentecostalism reckons baptism with the Spirit and anointing as the same experience. K E Abraham, founder of Indian Pentecostal Church, who was raised in the Syrian Christian Orthodox tradition in Kerala, and laid this doctrinal foundation since 1923 for the rapid Pentecostal church growth in India writes, "terms like Spirit-outpouring, Spirit-baptism, and Spirit-anointing are used interchangeably for the same experience."[241] It is significant to notice in contrast to the above assertions, there is a difference between "baptism in the Holy Spirit" and "anointing in the Holy Spirit." The terms are not to be used interchangeably because of the importance in both functions of the outpouring of the Spirit throughout history.

In the Old Testament, Priests, Kings, and the Prophets were anointed. Oil was poured on the head of the person being anointed (Exod. 29:7, 1 Sam. 15:1, 1 Kgs. 19:16). It was a sign of official appointment to office and a symbol of God's power.

Everyone in Christ needs the anointing which gives knowledge of the plan of God's redemptive and reconciliatory intervention as revealed in the scriptures (2 Cor. 1:20-21). Spiritual anointing resulted in the presence and favor of God. It was attested on Jesus' life and ministry. God anointed Jesus of Nazareth with the Holy Spirit and power, and He went around doing good and healing all who were under the power of the devil, because God was with Him (Acts 10:38). The Nazareth Manifesto was a bold declaration of Jesus in the context of Jewish religious domination which opposed any radical change to the existing rigid systems (Acts 4:28-29). Christian witness is not to be carried out merely with natural talents but with supernatural endowment. Jesus wanted the disciples to stay in the city until they had been clothed with power from on high as promised by the Father (Luke 24:49). This was not optional but mandatory for the disciples as Jesus repeated the command immediately before the ascension (Acts 1:5). The Holy Spirit would empower for Christian witness (Acts 1:8). The understanding that we are involved in a fully authorized enterprise is a central spiritual dynamic that gives confidence, boldness, and a sense of legitimate freedom in missions today. "We are not fishing without a license."[242]

---

[238] Jean Stone, in Hollenweger, 5.
[239] Donald W Dayton, *The Theological Roots of Pentecostalism*, (Metuchen, NJ and London: Scarecrow Press, 1987), 27.
[240] D Martyn Lloyd-Jones, *Baptism and Gifts of the Spirit*, (Grand Rapids: Baker Books, 1984, 1996), 421.
[241] K E Abraham, *Holy Spirit Baptism* (Language: Malayalam), (Kumbanad, Kerala: K E Abraham Foundation, 2011), 12.
[242] Douglas C McConnell (ed), *The Holy Spirit and Mission Dynamics*, (Pasadena, CA: William Carey Library, 1997), 13.

Why were the apostles so eager to bear witness to the resurrected Christ? Was it because of His resurrection appearances and the good news they have represented? Was it because of the Great Commission and the obligation of the mandate they represented? Or was it because of their Pentecostal experience? Though these factors contributed, the coming of the Spirit (anointing) must be identified as the central dynamic. Gary B McGee in "Surprises of the Holy Spirit: How Pentecostalism has Changed the Landscape of Modern Mission," writes, "successful evangelization required spirit filled missionaries in whose ministries displays of divine power would be the norm rather than the exception."[243]

The sound articulation of theology on anointing could guard the Church from unhealthy teaching that some people have special ability to impart special endowment of power to others. The anointing from God is a personal experience which is for the common benefit of the Church and for the expansion of His kingdom.

Scope: Anywhere to Everywhere and Anyone to Everyone

We are in the middle of one of the most dramatic demographic changes in the history of Christianity. Until recently, Christianity has been perceived to be a European and North American religion and identified almost exclusively with Western civilization. At the beginning of the 20th Century, 80 percent of the World's Christians lived in Europe and North America. However, as the Century closed, 60 percent of the World's Christians were living in Africa, Asia, and Latin America.[244] The pattern of migration from developing countries to the West made the Global South diverse in terms of religion, race, and culture. This happened because of wars, famines, political and military displacements, globalization, advancements made in education and technology, economic oppression, and related matters. We need to acknowledge that there is a major shift in the epi-center of Christianity, and the future of Christianity seems to lie not in the West but rather in the Non-western parts of the globe. One of the ironic features of the major shift taking place in World Christianity is the sudden and dramatic collapse of Christian faith among the Western Europeans. Quoted in "Mission from the Rest to the West," historian Callum Brown, in his book *The Death of Christian Britain*, describes how organized Christianity in Britain has been sent on "a downward spiral to the margins of social significance:"

In unprecedented numbers, the British people since the 1960s have stopped going to Church, have allowed their church membership to lapse, have stopped marrying in the Church, and have neglected to baptize their children. Meanwhile, their children, the two generations who grew to maturity in the last thirty years of the twentieth Century, stopped going to Sunday School, stopped entering confirmation or communicant classes, and rarely, if ever, stepped inside a Church to worship in their entire lives. The cycle which had, for so many centuries tied the people however closely or loosely to the churches and to Christian moral benchmarks, was permanently disrupted in the

---

[243] Gary B McGee, "Surprises of the Holy Spirit: How Pentecostalism has Changed the Landscape of Modern Mission," in Jonathan J Bonk (ed), *Between Past and Future: Evangelical Mission Entering the Twenty-first Century*, (Pasadena, CA: William Carey Library, 2003), 53.
[244] David B Barret, George T Kurien and Todd M Johnson (eds), *World Christian Encyclopedia*, 2nd ed. (New York: Oxford University Press, 2002).

swinging sixties. Since then, a formerly religious people have entirely forsaken organized Christianity in a sudden plunge into a truly secular condition.[245]

The Church loses 1500 people every week, losing people not only on the edge but also those at the heart of the Church, leaders and those involved for twenty to thirty years. This picture of the church and the society leads us to the need to formulate a Spirit-anointed witness that will emerge in a local context. The church is to be built up for vibrant worship under transformational worship instead of maintaining traditional spirituality with sacraments and intellectual, non-radical formulations of faith and practice. Global South Christians are far more conservative in terms of both beliefs and moral teachings. They hold fast to a strong supernatural orientation and are usually far more interested in personal salvation than in social justice issues and radical societal changes. The challenge for Christians is to have a worldview that subscribes to a belief in direct divine intervention in the daily lives of people. Peter Vethanayagamony writes in "Mission from the Rest to the West,"

The divine power that is mediated through Christianity can provide healing for mind, body, and soul, and these three entities of a person cannot be separated. Besides, the age-old local beliefs about visions, prophecy, and healing have also contributed to Christianity's distinctive Supernaturalism in the Global South.[246]

Instead of West to the Rest, the Rest to the West is the expectation of Christendom in the present decade.

The remedy for the decline of Christianity and failure in mission is to have Spirit-anointed witnesses with passion for the salvation of all in their own context. Missiology is an expanding and developing field of study to implement the findings related to cultures. Once cross-cultural meant everything related to cultures and missions; now, the term inter-cultural is introduced to one culture interacting with another in distinct cultural expressions, as in missions. Mission from anyone to everyone and anywhere to everywhere is to be practiced.

Enoch Wan introduced "Diaspora Missions" as a strategy in response to the reality of the demographic trend of diaspora. Diaspora missions include missions to the diaspora, missions through the diaspora, missions by and beyond the diaspora. These types of diaspora missions are carried out among various ethnic groups in different countries.[247]

The 10/40 window is to be given special attention for a Spirit-anointed witness. It is the area from 10 to 40 North of the equator, stretching from West Africa to Japan. The countries within the 10/40 window constitute only one-third of the earth's total land area, but account for two-thirds of the World's people. It encloses almost 100% of the World's 1.1 billion Muslims, 800 million Hindus, and 300 million Buddhists. The Window's nearly 4 billion residents include 97% of the inhabitants of the World's least evangelized nations. The 10/40 Window contains the birthplace of every major non-

---

[245] Callum Brown quoted in G Rosales and C G Arevalo (eds), *For all the People of Asia*, 1, (Manila: Claretian Publications, 1977, P130, Quoted by Peter Vethanayagamony, "Mission from the Rest to the West: The Changing Landscape of World Christianity and Christian Mission," in Ogbu U Kalu, Peter Vethanayagamony, Edmund Kee-Fook Chia (eds), *Mission After Christendom, Emergent Themes in Contemporary Mission*, (Louisville, KY: Westminister John Knox Press, 2010), 61.
[246] Kalu, Vethanayagamony, Kee-Fook Chia (eds), *Mission After Christendom*, 63.
[247] Enoch Wan, *Diaspora Missiology: Theory, Methodology, and Practice*, (Portland: Institute of Diaspora Studies, 2011), 185-189.

Christian religion on earth: Islam, Hinduism, Buddhism, Shintoism, Taoism, Confucianism, Bahai, Sikhism, Judaism, and Jainism.[248]

The Goal of Spirit-Anointed Witness: Worship
We find centuries of lifeless ritual in Christianity; the reformation was a turning point in bringing Bibles and hymnals for the congregation. A new awareness emerged to know, love, and serve God with the privilege for each person to read, meditate on, and interpret the Word of God. This is freedom in the Spirit everyone in Christ experiences, which has been a dream in the past. Becoming a worshipper is a privilege and a challenge everywhere.

Definition of Worship

Many attempts are made to define worship and no one definition seems to adequately express the fullness of worship – perhaps because worship is a divine encounter and so is as infinite in its depth as God Himself.[249] The English word worship comes from the Anglo-Saxon word *weorthscipe* which denotes one who is worthy of honor and reverence. In this sense, when we are worshipping God, we are declaring to Him His worth. In Revelation 4, the twenty-four elders worship the Lord by confessing that He is worthy to receive glory, honor, and power. The Hebrew word for worship is *Shaha*. It means to bow low or to prostrate oneself. The Greek word for worship is *proskuneo*, which literally means to kiss the hand of one who is revered. The New Testament concept of worship involves closeness and intimacy. The God Who was unapproachable under the Old Testament may be approached with boldness in the new covenant (Heb. 4:14-16). Here, worship is an expression of a love relationship.[250]

The Holy Spirit and Worship

The Holy Spirit is an integral part of our worship. Jesus was teaching a lesson from conversation with the Samaritan woman that God is Spirit, and His worshipers must worship in spirit and in truth (John 4:21-24). Samaritans worshipped in Mount Gerizim and the Jews worshipped in Jerusalem. Both failed to recognize the true worship pleasing to God. It would no longer be bound to a certain time or place, rather, it was going to be a function of the spirit of man responding to the Spirit of God. The Lord of heaven and earth doesn't live in temples built by human hands (Acts 17:24). Under the old covenant worship was a series of outward ceremonies where heart responses of the participants were not necessarily involved. God used sharp words against them: "These people come near to Me with their mouth and honor Me with their lips, but their hearts are far from Me. Their worship of Me is made up only of rules taught by men" (Isa. 29:13). So, true worship is to be distinguished from ignorant worship as well as hypocritical worship. True worship is through Jesus Christ, Who is the truth (John 14:6) the only mediator between God and man (1 Tim. 2:5). We have the perfect

[248] George Otis, Jr and Mark Brockman, *Strongholds of the 10/40 Window*, (Seattle, WA: YWAM Publishing, 1995), Back Cover Page.
[249] Bob Sorge, Exploring Worship: A Practical Guide to Praise and Worship, (Greenwood, MO: Oasis House, 2004) 63.
[250] Don McMinn, "The Power of Praise, Contemporary Worship, and Evangelism," in Beougher and Reid (eds), 68.

knowledge of God's revelation through Christ. When Christ is sanctified in hearts, worship is reflected in purity, integrity, and sincerity.

The four expressions known as prayer, worship, thanksgiving, and praise are very closely related or overlap with one another. We come across people who make the mistake of equating praise with worship. Worship is different because it is a two-way street, involving both giving and receiving. It is possible for praise to ascend one way only, however worship involves communion and fellowship. Praise is always seen or heard; worship is not always evident to an observer. Praise is largely horizontal in its purpose, while worship is primarily a vertical interaction. When we praise we speak to one another; and we declare His praise before one another. Worship may be more private and is much more preoccupied with the Godhead. Praise is often preparatory to worship or is conceived as a gateway to worship.[251]

Worship and Mission

Today as throughout history, worship and mission are linked inextricably together; for God propels His mission through the drawing of worshipers to Himself. God's call to worship Him empowers us to respond with His passion to do mission. The Samaritan woman encounters Jesus Christ, the incarnate God. He discloses that the Father is seeking authentic worshipers, people in relationship with Him. The woman responds by immediately calling others to come and see the Man Who told her everything she had done (John 4:28). The greatest call-and-response pattern surfaces when the disciples meet with the resurrected Jesus immediately before His ascension (Matt. 28:16ff). In recognizing Jesus' true identity, they worshipped Him. In the context of worship, Jesus gives His crowning imperative, the Great Commission (Matt. 28:17-20). The missionary mandate flows out of an intimate relationship with God, generated in worship. We join Him in His passion to call worshippers to Himself.[252]

Worship is a powerful witness to unbelievers if God's presence is felt and if the message is understandable. On the day of Pentecost (Acts 2) God's presence was evident in the worship service so that it attracted the attention of a large crowd and 3000 people were saved that day. It is God's presence that melts hearts and explodes mental barriers. Rick Warren writes, "In genuine worship God's presence is felt, God's pardon is offered, God's purposes are revealed, and God's power is displayed."[253]

John Piper writes, "Mission is not the ultimate goal of the Church, Worship is. Worship is ultimate, not missions, because God is ultimate, not man."[254] The glory of God is to be the ultimate goal of everything. God created everything for His glory. The heavens declare the glory of God and the sky above proclaims His handiwork (Ps. 19:1). The vision of the prophet Isaiah on Angelic worship reveals "Holy, Holy, Holy, the LORD of hosts; the whole earth is full of His glory" (Isa. 6:3). Human sin is fundamentally a failure to live up to the glory of that image and to give God the glory that naturally belongs to Him (cf. Rom. 3:23). Idolatry is the foolish exchange of the true glory of the living God for

---

[251] Sorge, 67-70.
[252] Roberta R King, "Worship," in Scott A Moreau, Harold Netland, and Charles Van Engen (eds), *Evangelical Dictionary of World Missions*, (Grand Rapids: Baker Books, 2005), 1034.
[253] Rick Warren, The Purpose Driven Church: Growth Without Compromising Your Message and Mission, (Grand Rapids: Zondervan, 1995), 242.
[254] John Piper, Let the Nations Be Glad: The Supremacy of God in Missions, (Grand Rapids: Baker Books, 1993), 11.

the shoddy false glory of man-made gods (Rom. 1:22-23). Paul argues that the final objective of the work of the Triune God in redeeming fallen people is the praise of His glory (Eph. 1:3-14). The destiny of the creation is universal knowledge of the glory of God: "For the earth will be filled with the knowledge of the glory of the LORD as the waters cover the sea" (Hab. 2:14). Zane Pratt, in "The Heart of Mission: Redemption," writes, "The mission of God has the glory of God as its driving passion and as its ultimate goal, as God reveals the amazing spectrum of His glory in creation, judgement, redemption, and restoration."[255]

There is an intimate connection between worship and mission. The result of Isaiah's powerful worship experience (Isa. 6:1-8) saying, "Here am I send me" shows us true worship causes true mission. Paul also highlighted the glorious picture of worship in his Christological hymn, "At the name of Jesus every knee shall bow in heaven and on earth and every tongue confess that Jesus Christ is Lord to the glory of God the Father" (Phil. 2:10-11). The goal of Spirit-anointed witness in Christian mission leads everyone to behold the glory of God. William Temple writes, "to worship is to quicken the conscience by the holiness of God, to feed the mind with the truth of God, to purge the imagination by the beauty of God, to open the heart by the love of God, and devote the will to the purpose of God."[256]

God's call to worship Him is currently sweeping around the World in great, new revolutionary ways. Along with new openness to new forms and patterns of worship, there is greater recognition of the intimate relationship between worship and mission. According to Roberta R King, "Research reveals that where dynamic worship is practiced, changed lives and growing churches resulted. Worship forms are shaped by and reflect our relationship with God via appropriate, expressive cultural forms. There is a great need for openness in pursuing, experimenting, exchanging, and documenting experiences in worship."

Authentic Christian worship brings people to encounter Jesus Christ. As one looks to God, God reveals His vision to Him. We respond to this call. Thus, worship propels and empowers vision. Ultimately, God calls us to participate in achieving God's vision as intoned by the Psalmist: All the nations you have made will come and worship before you, O Lord; they will bring glory to your name.[257]

Christian worship is not confined to Sunday-morning services, rather it is glorifying God with others, integrating all elements in worship by acknowledging the supremacy and glory of God in every realm of life. Spirit-anointed worship and witness are inextricably interwoven which must be given priority in mission practice.

---

[255] Zane Pratt, "The Heart of Mission: Redemption," in Ashford (ed), 49.
[256] William Temple, in James K Bridges, "Making Place for Pentecostal Distinctives," in Trask, Bicket, and Goodall (eds), 550.
[257] King, in Moreau, Netland, and Van Engen (eds), 1035.

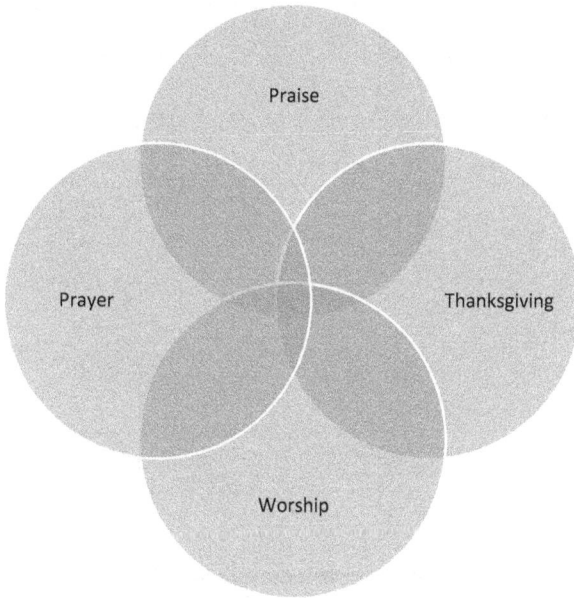

Figure 6: Integration of Expressions in Worship[258]
The diagram above serves our readers well by showing visibly the integration of expressions in worship.

Summary

The Scope in Spirit-anointed witness in holistic mission is understood as anywhere to everywhere and anyone to everyone. The "unreached" is not at a distance but in the neighborhood or at the backyard of every Christian witness. Every heart without Christ is the mission field. The goal in the Spirit-anointed witness is to lead everyone to behold the glory of God. We should be shaped in our thinking and our living by a vision of Holy God being worshipped and honored through Christ by the Holy Spirit.

---

[258] Sorge, 68.

CHAPTER 7
CONCLUSION

This book is an attempt to articulate a theology of Spirit-anointed witness in a context where the role of Holy Spirit has been misunderstood and misinterpreted. There are many theologians and missiologists who claim to be Trinitarian in perspective yet sideline the Holy Spirit, giving Father and Son superior status. This volume is an effort to restore Bible based, God honored, Christ centered, and Spirit-guided Christian theology and witness in the 21st Century.

First, a holistic focus for Christian mission has been developed and affirmed in this research. Key verses selected for exegetical study are Luke 4:18-19, 24:46-49, Acts 1:0, 10:38, Matthew 28:18-20, and Romans 15:17-20 which provide basic missiological implications for Mission in our context. The Nazareth Manifesto in the Lucan narrative guides us to have an integration of spiritual, physical, social, and psychological spheres of human life yet with a priority of spiritual deliverance in Christian witness. Pauline focus is also narrated well in passion for proclaiming the Word accompanied with signs and wonders and compassionate service to the needy in his ministry.

Second, the relational paradigm fits well in this theological development. Relationship is foundational in Christian mission and a pre-requisite to the articulation of theology and missiology. The pattern of relational function in the Trinity, where knowledge of one another, unity of will, and expression of love are evident, becomes the model for Christian mission. We are to promote loving relationships in a community where people are segregated by class, race, caste, language, religion, ideology, etc. The vertical relationship is foundational and the horizontal is to be built upon it. The solution for disharmony in an individual, family, society at micro and macro levels is to realize and affirm the loving relationship.

Third, the theology of Spirit-anointed witness in holistic Christian mission resulted from study and reflection on the two major supernatural events in history: Christ-event and Spirit-event. Christ-event is the corner stone in Christian theology and mission. Christ-event is the foundation in which incarnation, death, resurrection, exaltation, and imminent return of Christ are significant concepts for an anointed witness. Christian faith and message of a missionary is focused on the work God has done through Jesus Christ rather than on the works we do. God's grace and love are demonstrated in all events destined by God for the salvation of those who believe in His Lordship and Saviorhood. It is re-affirming the reformation perspectives in soteriology.

Fourth, it is significant to restore the experiential aspect of Christian life and witness which is true to the scripture. Spirit-event has the dynamic anchor role in Christian theology and missional practice. This research is intended to make an awareness of the difference between "baptism in the Holy Spirit" and "anointing in the Holy Spirit." Baptism in the Spirit is an act of Jesus Christ enabling a believer to realize the unity and oneness of the body of Christ, however, anointing in the Holy Spirit is an act of God for authorizing, enriching, enlightening, empowering, and equipping a person to proclaim, practice, and demonstrate the power of God's Kingdom (Spirit-anointed witness). This is a position toward a heart-oriented praxis that fully embraces a supernatural worldview. Eastern Churches under traditional bias are content with symbolism and sacraments. The western church under great pressure from rationalism and a science-oriented society through the years, has failed to practice a theology of the Spirit realm.

Fifth, "Spiritual warfare" is recognized as a reality because it is found in the Old and the New Testaments. Jesus Christ, confronted, could overcome the challenges by the Holy Spirit. This is true with us in the mission field where numerous people are tormented by demonic forces. Neglecting the challenge is a failure because these tormented people could look at pastors and mission practitioners for emergency help in their crisis. The Sprit-anointed minister could carry out a deliverance ministry out of compassion and love. On the other side there are many who manipulate in their ministry for selfish motives and bring damage to Christianity. Christ in us is greater than the one who is in the World (1 John 4:4).

Sixth, Church in the World has a tremendous role to witness the Kingdom of God. Church and the Kingdom are not the same. The Kingdom of God is understood as the reign of God. The eschatological framework of the Kingdom as both "now and not yet" provides theological basis for holistic mission globally. The church exists "between the times" – between the inauguration and the consummation of the Kingdom. Church is to be empowered by the Holy Spirit for the Kingdom. The question by the disciples to Jesus concerning the restoration of the Kingdom to Israel will be fulfilled in the future. Church looks forward to the imminent return of Jesus Christ and needs to focus on the Kingdom of God. Jesus' words, "My Kingdom is not of this world...but, now My Kingdom is from another place" (John 18:36) is a clear expression against the social Gospel and human ideologies engaged in promoting the kingdom as only a present reality.

Seventh, the ministry of reconciliation is entrusted to the church because church is a reconciled community. The Christ-event and the Spirit-event are the foundation for reconciliation. Reconciliation through Jesus Christ is the message of Christian witness. The one reconciled unto God will desire to reconcile with others. The vertical and horizontal aspects of reconciliation bring remedy for the conflicts. Forgiveness and repentance are significant in the message of reconciliation.

Eighth, effective Christian witness is based on the right methods employed. Jesus Christ used various methods in communicating the values and power of God's Kingdom. Spirit-anointing involves guidance for effective ways to reach the unreached. Message and method are to be well connected in mission.

Ninth, the scope, "anyone to everyone and anywhere to everywhere," really transforms the missional perspective of the Church. Diaspora missiology is to be well integrated in Spirit-anointed witness. Church as a community of faith and fellowship needs to realize the dynamic participation in Mission primarily in where we are. Nations have come to the major cities of the World. This will bring a shift from homogeneous to multi-cultural in perspective for witness and worship.

Lastly, "To God be the glory" should be the goal of a missionary. We need to earnestly engage in Spirit-anointed witness to see reconciled people offer praise and worship before the holy God. "Whatever you do, work at it with all your heart, as working for the Lord, not for man" (Col. 3:23). It motivates us for faithful witness in Christian stewardship.

As Timothy Tennent writes, increasingly, mission practice in the World understands the book of Acts not only as an accurate description of the Holy Spirit's work through the early church but also as a prescriptive paradigm that should guide the church's practice today.[259]

Motivation and passion for doing more research on topics have emerged, topics such as Christian witness in a dialogical context, relational paradigm, and the role of seminaries in the formation of anointed ministers in a holistic-diaspora missiological context. More awareness needs to occur among the ministers of the churches to have a united effort in equipping people for the imminent return of Christ.

A theology of Spirit-anointed witness in Christian holistic mission may become a corrective reflection in the context of materialism, secularization, universalism, post-modernism, and religious persecution which are challenges in the World.

---

[259] Tennent, 428.

BIBLIOGRAPHY

Abraham, K E. *Holy Spirit Baptism* (Language: Malayalam). Kumbanad, Kerala: K E Abraham Foundation, 2011.

Aghamkar, Atul. *Mission in the Metropolis: Towards a Contextual Missiology for Urban India.* Sabbatical Research Proposal. (Accessed January 1, 2018).

Anderson, Norman. *The Mystery of the Incarnation.* Downers Grove: InterVarsity Press, 1979.

An Indian Christian. Percentage of Christians in India, 2013.
    http://anindianchristian.blogspot.com/2013/01/percentage-of-christians-in-india.html
    (Accessed February 28, 2018).

Ashford, Bruce Riley (ed). *Theology and Practice of Mission: God, the Church, and the Nations.* Nashville, TN: B&H Publishing Group, 2011.

Barret, David B, George T Kurien and Todd M Johnson (eds). *World Christian Encyclopedia* 2nd ed. New York, Oxford: University Press, 2002.

Beilby, James K and Paul R Eddy (eds). *The Nature of the Atonement: Four Views.* Downers Grove: IVP Academic, 2006.

Beougher, Timothy and Alvin Reid (eds). *Evangelism for a Changing World: Essays in Honor of Roy J Fish.* Wheaton: Harold Shaw Publishers, 1995.

Bible Society of India. *History of Translations: The First Bible to be Translated in India.* www.bsind.org/tamil_bible_translations.html (Accessed December 12, 2017).

Billings, Todd. "The Problem with Incarnational Ministry." *Christianity Today*, July-August 2012, 60.

Birkey, Del. *The House Church: A Model of Renewing the Church.* Scottdale, PA: Herald Press, 1988, 1993.

Bock, Darrel L. *The NIV Application Commentary.* Grand Rapids: Zondervan Publishing, 1996.

Bock, Darrel L and Andreas Kostenberger (eds). *A Theology of Luke and Acts: Biblical Theology of the New Testament.* Grand Rapids: Zondervan, 2012.

Boehme, Ron. *The Fourth Wave: Taking Your Place in the New Era of Missions.* Seattle, WA: YWAM Publishing, 2011.

Boer, Harry R. *Pentecost and Missions.* Grand Rapids: Eerdmans Publishing, 1961.

Bonhoeffer, Dietrich. *The Cost of Discipleship,* New York: Touch Stone, 1995.

Bonk, Jonathan J (ed). *Between Past and Future: Evangelical Mission Entering the Twenty-first Century.* Pasadena, CA: William Carey Library, 2003.

Borthwick, Paul. *Great Commission, Great Compassion: Following Jesus and Loving the World.* Downers Grove: IVP Books, 2015.

Bosch, David J. *Transforming Mission: Paradigm Shifts in Theology of Mission.* Maryknoll, NY: Orbis Books, 1991.

_____. *Witness to the World: The Christian Mission in Theological Perspective.* Atlanta: John Knox Press, 1980.

Brand, Chad Owen. *Perspectives on Spirit Baptism: Five Views.* Nashville: B&H Academic, 2004.

Briscoe, Pete and Todd Hillard. *The Surge: Churches Catching the Wave of Christ's Love for the Nations.* Grand Rapids: Zondervan, 2010.

Brown, C (ed). *New International Dictionary of the New Testament.* Exeter: Paternoster, 1976.

Brunner, Frederick Dale. *A Theology of the Holy Spirit: The Pentecostal Experience and New Testament Witness.* Eugene, OR: Wipf and Stock Publishers, 1997.

Casey, Anthony. *A New Reality: Charles Kraft's View of Spiritual Warfare.* https://culturncity.files.wordpress.com/2011/04/kraft-on-spiritual-warfare.pdf (Accessed December 10, 2017).

Chawla, Navin. "Conscience-keeper of her century: Mother Theresa dedicated her life to alleviating hunger and destitution." Published August 2013. http://www.dailymail.co.uk/indiahome/indianews/article-2401120/Mother-Theresa-dedicated-life-alleviating-loneliness-hunger-destitution.html (Accessed October 29, 2017).

Chiaramonte, Perry. "Christians the Most Persecuted Group in the World." *Fox News*, January 06, 2017.

Clark, David K. *To Know and Love God.* Wheaton: Crossway, 2003.

Clark, John C and Marcus Peter Johnson. *The Incarnation of God: The Ministry of the Gospel as the Foundation of Evangelical Theology.* Wheaton: Crossway, 2015.

Coldiron, James D. "Spiritual Warfare Basics." 2004. http://www.voiceofthewatchman.org/audio/Spiritual%20Warfare%20Basics.htm (Accessed November 2017).

Cole, Graham Arthur. *The God Who Became Human: A Biblical Theology of Incarnation.* Downers Grove: InterVarsity Press, 2013.

Costas, Orlando. *The Integrity of Mission: The Inner Life and Outreach of the Church.* San Francisco: Harper and Row, 1979.

Cox, Harvey. *Fire from Heaven: The Rise of Pentecostal Spirituality and the Reshaping of Religion in the 21st Century.* Addison-Wesley Publishing Company, 1994.

Creswell, John W. *Quality Inquiry and Research Design.* Los Angeles, CA: SAGE Publications, 2013.

Darko, Daniel K and Beth Snodderly (eds). *First the Kingdom of God: Global Voices on Global Mission.* Pasadena, CA: William Carey International University Press, 2014.

Dayton, Donald W. *The Theological Roots of Pentecostalism.* Metuchen, NJ and London: Scarecrow Press, 1987.

Dempster, Murray W, Byron D Klaus, and Douglas Petersen (eds). *Called & Empowered: Global Mission in Pentecostal Perspective.* Peabody, MA: Hendrickson Publishers, 1991.

Denyer, Simon. "Jesus won't save you – President Xi Jinping will, Chinese Christians told." (Accessed November 15, 2017).

Ditmanson, Harold H. *Grace in Experience and Theology.* Minneapolis: Augsburg Publishing House, 1977.

Dodd, C H. *The Parables of the Kingdom.* London: Nisbet, 1935.

Dowsett, Rose. *The Great Commission.* Mill Hill, London and Grand Rapids: Monarch Books, 2001.

Dunn, James D G. *Christology in the Making: A New Testament Inquiry into the Origins of the Doctrine and Incarnation*. Grand Rapids: Eerdmans Publishing, 1989.

Early, Patrick Alexander. *Articulating the Doctrine of Penal Substitution Atonement in the 21st Century: Integrating Relational Paradigm with the Metaphor of Kaleidoscope*. Unpublished Dissertation, Western Seminary, Portland, April 2017.

Eckward, Paul J. *The Missionary: Realities, Strategy, and Methods*. Downers Grove: IVP Academic, 2008.

Elliston, Edgar J. *Introduction to Missiological Research Design*. Pasadena: William Carey, 2011

Erickson, Millard J. *Christian Theology*. Grand Rapids: Baker House, 1986.

Fee, Gordon D. *God's Empowering Presence: The Holy Spirit in the Letters of Paul*. Peabody, MA: Hendrickson Publishers, 1994.

Geisler, Norman L. *Systematic Theology, vol 2*. Minneapolis: Bethany House, 2003.

Geisler, Norman L and Chad V Meister (eds). *Reasons for Faith: Making a Case for Christian Faith*. Wheaton: Crossway Books, 2007.

Geisler, Norman L and Paul K Hoffman (eds). *Why I Am a Christian?* Grand Rapids: Baker Books, 2001.

George, Sam. *Understanding the Coconut Generation*. Niles, IL: Mall Publishing 2006.

Gilliand, Anne. "Archival Research Methods." Published September 2011. http://ozk.unizd.hr/summerschool2011/wp-content/uploads/2011/06/Gilliland_Archival-Research-Methods.pdf (Accessed October 16, 2017).

Glasser, Arthur F and Donald A McGavran (eds). *Contemporary Theology of Mission*. Grand Rapids: Baker Books, 1983.

Global Ministries: The United Methodist Church. "Bible Translation as Mission." http://www.umcmission.org/Learn-About-Us/News-and-Stories/2011/May/Bible-Translation-as-Mission (Accessed September 15, 2017).

Gnanakan, Ken R. *Kingdom Concerns: A Biblical Exploration Towards a Theology of Mission*. Bangalore, India: Theological Book Trust, 1989.

Goheen, Michael W. *Introducing Christian Mission Today: Scripture, History and Issues*. Downers Grove: IVP Academic, 2014.

Gopakumar, R. *Indian Diaspora and Giving Patterns of Indian Americans in the USA*. New Delhi, India: Charities Aid Foundation, 2003.

Graham, Billy. *The Inspirational Writings*. New York: Inspirational Press, 1995.

_____. *Just as I Am: The Autobiography of Billy Graham*. New York: Harper Collins, 2007.

Green, Michael. *I Believe in The Holy Spirit*. Grand Rapids: William B Eerdmans Publishing, 1975.

Greenway, Roger S. *Go and Make Disciples: An Introduction to Christian Missions*. Philipsburg: NJ: P&R Publishing, 1996, 1999.

Hargreave, John A. *A Guide to Acts*, Delhi: ISPCK, 1990.

Harris, R Geoffrey. *Mission in the Gospels*. Eugene, OR: Wipf and Stock, 2004.

Harvey, John D. *Anointed with the Spirit and Power: The Holy Spirit Empowering Presence*. New Jersey: RR Publishing, 2008.

Henderson, David W. *Culture Shift: Communicating God's Truth in a Changing World*. Grand Rapids: Baker House, 1978, 1998.

Hendricksen, William and Simon J Kistemaker. *Luke.* New Testament Commentary. Grand Rapids: Baker Academic, 1978.

Hendry, George S. *The Gospel of the Incarnation.* Philadelphia: Westminister Press, 1959.

Hesselgrave, David. *Theology and Mission: Papers and Responses Prepared for the Consultation on Theology and Mission, Trinity Evangelical Divinity School, School of World Mission and Evangelism, March 22-25, 1976.* Grand Rapids: Baker Books, 1978.

Hick, John. *God has Many Names.* Philadelphia: Westminister Press, 1982.

Hiebert, Paul G. *The Gospel in Human Contexts.* Grand Rapids, MI: Baker Academic, 2009.

Hollenweger, W J. *The Pentecostals: The Charismatic Movement in the Churches.* Minneapolis: Augsburg Publishing, 1972.

Horner, David. *When Missions Shapes the Mission: You and Your Church Can Reach the World.* Nashville, TN: B&H Publishing, 2011.

Horrobin, Peter. *Healing through Deliverance: The Practice of Deliverance Ministry, vol. 2.* Grand Rapids: Chosen Books, 1991.

Hughes, Dewi. "Introduction to Holistic Mission," *Occasional Paper,* no 33 Pattaya Lausanne Committee for World Evangelization, 2005.

Jeffrey, Steve, Michael Ovey and Andrew Sach. *Pierced for Our Transgressions: Rediscovering the Glory of Penal Substitution.* Nottingham, PA: IVP, 2017.

Johnston, Thomas P (ed). *Mobilizing a Great Commission Church for Harvest.* Eugene, OR: Wipf and Stock, 2011.

Joshi, Aakash. "Remembering Graham Staines, 17 Years After His Murder." *The Quint,* Published January 2017. https://www.thequint.com/news/india/remembering-graham-staines-17-years-after-his-murder (Accessed December 12, 2017).

Kalu, Ogbu U, Peter Vethanayagamony, Edmund Kee-Fook Chia (eds). *Mission After Christendom: Emergent Themes in Contemporary Mission.* Louisville, KY: Westminster John Knox Press, 2010.

Kane, Herbert J. *The Christian World Mission: Today and Tomorrow.* Grand Rapids: Baker House, 1981.

Karkkainen, Veli-Matti. *Toward a Pneumatological Theology.* Maryland, USA: University Press of America, 2002.

Kelly, J N D. *Early Christian Doctrines.* New York: Harper and Row, 1960.

Kendal, R T. *The Anointing: Yesterday, Today and Tomorrow.* Florida: Charisma House 2003.

Kim, Kirsteen. "The Reconciling Spirit: The Dove with Color and Strength." *The International Review of Missions* vol 94, no 372 (January 2005), 21-22.

Kostenberger, Andreas J. *The Missions of Jesus and the Disciples According to the Fourth Gospel.* Grand Rapids: Eerdmans Publishing, 1998.

Kostenberger, Andreas J and Peter T O'Brien. *Salvation to the Ends of the Earth: A Biblical Theology of Mission.* Downers Grove, IL: InterVarsity Press, 2011.

Kraft, Charles. *Christianity in Culture: A Study in Dynamic, Biblical Theologizing in Cross-Cultural Perspective.* Maryknoll, NY: Orbis Books, 1979.

_____. *Christianity with Power: Your Worldview and Your Experience of the Supernatural.* Ann Arbor: Servant Books, 1989.

_____. *Confronting Powerless Christianity: Evangelicals and the Missing Dimension*. Grand Rapids: Chosen Books, 2002.

_____. *Defeating Dark Angels: Breaking Demonic Oppression in the Believer's Life*. Ann Arbor: Servant Publications, 1992.

Kraft, Marguerite G, *Understanding Spiritual Power*. Maryknoll, NY: Orbis Books, 1995.

Kraus, Norman C. *Missions, Evangelism, and Church Growth*. Scottdale, PA: Herald Press, 1980.

Krodel, Gerhard A. *Acts*, Augsburg Commentary on the New Testament. Minneapolis: Augsburg Publishing House, 1986.

Ladd, George Elden. *A Theology of the New Testament*. Grand Rapids: William Eerdmans Publishing, 1974.

Larkin, William J Jr and Grant R Osborne. *Acts*. Downers Grove, IL: IVP Academic, 1995.

Latourette, Kenneth Scott. *A History of Christianity*. Peabody, MA: Prince Press, 2000.

Lausanne Global Analysis. *Number of Christians in China and India*, 2012. http://www.lausanne.org/lgc-transfer/number-of-christians-in-china-and-india-2 (Accessed February 28, 2018).

Lee, Edgar R. "Living in the Presence of God: A Theology of Spiritual Formation." *Enrichment Journal*, Summer 2002. http:/enrichmentjournal.ag.org/200203/200203_086_sptformation.cfm (Accessed September 10, 2017).

Leithart, Peter J. *The Kingdom and the Power: Rediscovering the Centrality of the Church*. Phillipsburg, NJ: P&R Publishing, 1993.

Letham Robert. *The Work of Christ: Contours of Christian Theology*. Downers Grove: InterVarsity Press, 1993.

Lim, Johnson T K (ed). *Holy Spirit: Unfinished Agenda*. Singapore: Genesis Books and Word N Works, 2015.

Lloyd-Jones, D Martyn. *Baptism and Gifts of the Holy Spirit*. Grand Rapids: Baker Books, 1984, 1996.

_____. *God's Way of Reconciliation: Ephesians 2:1-22*. Edinburgh: Banner of Truth, 1981.

Lukos, Saji. *Kingdom Perspective: Lessons Learned to Impact Our World*. Huntley, IL: Mall Publishing, 2016.

_____. *Transformed for a Purpose*. Huntley, IL: Mall Publishing, 2016.

Lundy, David. *Borderless Church: Shaping the Church for the 21st Century*. Bletchley, UK: Authentic Media, 2005.

MacAlpine, Thomas H. *By Word, Work, and Wonder: Cases in Holistic Mission*. Monrovia, CA: MARC, 1995.

Macchia, Frank. *Baptized in the Spirit: A Global Pentecostal Theology*. Grand Rapids: Zondervan, 2006.

Maune, Michael, Nicholas Marino, and Gina Hurley. "Introduction to Archives." https://owl.english.purdue.edu/owl/resource/988/1 (Accessed November 23, 2017).

McConnell, Douglas C (ed). *The Holy Spirit and Mission Dynamics*. Pasadena, CA: William Carey Library, 1997.

McDowell, Sean. *A New Kind of Apologist: Adopting Fresh Strategies, Addressing the Latest Issues, Engaging the Culture*. Eugene, OR: Harvest House Publishers, 2016.

McGavran, Donald A. *Understanding Church Growth*, 3rd ed. Grand Rapids: Eerdmans, 1990.

McGee, J Vernon. *Revelation Chapters 1-5,* Thru the Bible Commentary Series. Nashville: Thomas Nelson Publishers, 1991.

McGrath, Alister. *Understanding Jesus: Who Jesus Christ Is and Why He Matters.* Grand Rapids, MI: Academic Books, 1987.

Menzies, Robert P. *Pentecostalism in Context: Essays in Honor of William W. Menzies.* Sheffield, UK: Sheffield Academic Press, 1997.

Miller, Lisa. "We Are All Hindus Now." *Newsweek,* August 15, 2009.

Moreau, Scott A. *Contextualization in World Missions: Mapping and Assessing Evangelical Models,* Grand Rapids: Kregel Academic, 2012.

Moreau, Scott A, Gary R Corvin and Gary B McGee (eds). *Introducing World Missions: A Biblical, Historical, and Practical Survey.* Grand Rapids: Baker Academic, 2004.

Moreau, Scott A, Harold Netland and Charles Van Engen (eds). *Evangelical Dictionary of World Missions.* Grand Rapids: Baker Books, 2005.

Morgan, Christopher W and Robert A Peterson (eds). *The Deity of Christ.* Wheaton: Crossway, 2011.

Morris, Leon. *The Cross in the New Testament.* Grand Rapids: Eerdmans Publishing, 1972.

Newbigin, Lesslie. *The Household of God.* London: SCM Press, 1953.

Neumann, Peter D. *Pentecostal Experience: An Ecumenical Encounter.* Eugene, OR: Pickwick Publication, 2012.

Ockenga, Harold John. *Power Through Pentecost.* Grand Rapids: Eerdmans Publishing, 1959.

Ogbu, Kalu U, Peter Vethanayagamony and Edmund Kee-Fook Chia (eds). *Mission After Christendom: Emergent Themes in Contemporary Mission.* Louisville, KY: Westminster John Knox Press, 2010.

Orr, James. *The Resurrection of Jesus.* Eugene, OR: Wipf and Stock Publishers, 1997.

Ott, Craig and J D Payne (eds). *Missionary Methods: Research, Reflections, and Realities.* Pasadena: William Carey Library, 2013.

Ott, Craig, Stephen J Strauss, Timothy C Tennent (eds). *Encountering Theology of Mission.* Grand Rapids: Baker Academic, 2010.

Otis, George Jr and Mark Brockman. *Strongholds of the 10/40 Window.* Seattle, WA: YWAM Publishing, 1995.

Padilla, Rene. "The Unity of the Church and the Homogeneous Unit Principle." *International Bulletin of Missionary Research* 6, no 1 (1982), 23-30.

Paterson, Tom. *Deeper, Richer, Fuller: Discover the Spiritual Life You Long For.* New York: Howard Books, 2010.

Pelican, Jaroslav. *The Christian Tradition.* Chicago: University of Chicago, 1971.

Perry, Lloyd M & Norman Shawchuck. *Revitalizing the Twentieth Century Church.* Chicago: Moody Press, 1982, 1986.

Peterson, D G (ed). *The Word Became Flesh: Evangelicals and the Incarnation.* Carlisle: Paternoster, 2003.

Pew Research Forum, *Asian Americans: A Mosaic of Faiths.* http://www.pewforum.org/2012/07/19/Asian-americans-a-mosaic-of-faiths-overview (Accessed October 13, 2014).

Piper, John. *Let the Nations Be Glad: The Supremacy of God in Missions.* Grand Rapids: Baker Books, 1993.

Polhill, John B. *Acts*, The New American Commentary vol 26. Nashville, TN: Broadman Press, 1992.

Purves, Andrew. *Exploring Christology and Atonement*. Downers Grove: IVP Academic, 2015.

Rainer Thom S (ed). *Evangelism in the Twenty-first Century: The Critical Issues*. Wheaton: Harold Shaw Publishers, 1989.

Rayburn, Robert. "Baptism of the Holy Spirit and the Second Blessing." http://reformedperspectives.org/articles/rob_rayburn/rob_rayburn.Acts19.1_7.html (Accessed December 15, 2017).

Rea, John. *The Holy Spirit in the Bible: A Commentary*. Lake Mary, FL: Creation House, 1990.

Rosales, G and C G Arevalo (eds). *For All the People of Asia*. Manila: Claretian Publication, 1977.

Ryrie, Charles. *Balancing the Christian Life*. Chicago: Moody Publishers, 1994.

Samartha, Stanley J. "The Holy Spirit and People of Other Faiths." *Ecumenical Review* 42.3-4 (1990), 250-263.

Samuel, Vinay and Albrecht Hauser. *Proclaiming Christ in Christ's Way: Studies in Integral Mission: Essays Presented to Walter Arnold on the Occasion of His 60th Birthday*. Eugene, OR: Wipf and Stock, 2007.

Samuel, Vinay and Chris Sugden. *Mission as Transformation: A Theology of the Whole Gospel*, Oxford: Regnum Books, 1999.

Schanbel, Eckhard J. *Paul the Missionary: Realities, Strategies, and Methods*. Downers Grove: IVP Academic, 2008.

Schmiechen, Peter. *Saving Power: Theories of Atonement and Forms of the Church*. Grand Rapids: Eerdmans Publishing, 2005.

Seamands, John T. *Tell it Well: Communicating the Gospel Across Cultures*. Kansas City: Beacon Hill Press, 1981.

Sebba, Anne. *Mother Teresa: Beyond the Image*. New York: Doubleday, 1998.

Shenk, Wilbert R (ed). *The Transfiguration of Mission: Biblical, Theological, and Historical Foundations*. Scottdale, PA: Herald Press, 1993.

Simpson, A B. "The Fourfold Gospel." https://www.cmalliance.org/about/beliefs/fourfold-Gospel (Accessed September 28, 2017).

Singh, Sadhu Sundar. *Reality and Religion: Meditations on God, Man, and Nature*. Madras: Christian Literature Service, 1974.

Slick, Matt. "Is the Lord a God of Peace or War?" https://carm.org/lord-god-peace-or-war (Accessed December 10, 2017).

Sorge, Bob. *Exploring Worship: A Practical Guide to Praise and Worship*. Greenwood, MO: Oasis House, 2004.

Stephen, M (ed). *Faith and Praxis: Essays and Reflections in Honor of Rev Dr T G Koshy*. Manakala, Kerala, India: Faith Theological Seminary, 2012.

Stetzer, Ed and David Hesselgrave (eds). *Mission Shift: Global Mission Issues in the Third Millennium*. Nashville: B&H Publishing Group, 2010.

Stetzer, Ed and David Putman. *Breaking the Missional Code*. Nashville: Broadman & Holman Publishers, 2006.

Stott, John R W. *Christian Mission in the Modern World*. Downers Grove: InterVarsity Press, 1975.

_____. *The Cross of Christ*. Leicester, UK: InterVarsity, 2006.

_____. *Your Mind Matters*. Downers Grove: InterVarsity Press, 1972.

Stott, John R W and Christopher Wright. *Christian Mission in the Modern World*. Downers Grove: InterVarsity Press, 2015.

Sunquist, Scott W. *Understanding Christian Mission: Participating in Suffering and Glory*. Grand Rapids: Baker Academic, 2013.

Swindol, Charles and Roy B Zuck (eds). *Understanding Christian Theology*. Nashville: Thomas Nelson Publishers, 2003.

Synan, Vinson. *In the Latter Days: The Outpouring of the Holy Spirit in the Twentieth Century*. Michigan: Servant Books, 1984.

Tennent, Timothy C. *Introduction to World Missions: A Trinitarian Missiology for the Twenty-First Century*. Grand Rapids: Kregel Academy Publications, 2010.

Terry, John Mark, Ebbie Smith, and Justice Anderson (eds). *Missiology: An Introduction to the Foundations, History, and Strategies of World Missions*. Nashville: Broadman & Holman Publishers, 1998.

Thomas, Norman E. *Missions and Unity: Lessons from History 1792 – 2010*. Eugene, OR: Cascade Books, 2010.

Thomas, Norman E (ed). *Classic Texts in World Mission and Christianity*. New York: Orbis Books, 1995.

Torrance, Thomas F. *Atonement: The Person and Work of Christ*. Downers Grove, IL: IVP Academic, 2009.

Torres, Hazel. "Christians Packing Churches in India as Christianity Sees Surprising Growth Despite Rising Persecution Cases." https://www.christiantoday.com/article/christians-packing-churches-in-india-as-christianity-sees-surprising-growth-despite-rising-persecution-cases/99915.htm

Torrey, R A. *Power-Filled Living: How to Receive God's Best for Your Life*. New Kensington. PA: Whitaker House, 1999.

Trask, Thomas E, Zenas J Bicket, and Wayde I Goodall (eds). *The Pentecostal Pastor: A Mandate for the 21st Century*. Springfield, MO: Gospel Publishing House, 2003.

Tucker, Ruth A. *A Biographical History of Christian Missions*, Grand Rapids: Baker House, 1983.

Turner, Max. *Power from On High: The Spirit in Israel's Restoration and Witness in Luke – Acts*. Sheffield: Sheffield Academic Press, 1996.

_____. *The Holy Spirit and Spiritual Gifts*. Peabody, MA: Hendrickson Publishers, 1996.

Twelftree, Graham. *People of the Spirit: Exploring Luke's View of the Church*. (Grand Rapids: Baker Academic, 2009.

Tyra, Gary. *The Holy Spirit in Mission*. Downers Grove: IVP Academic, 2011.

Van Engen, Charles. *Mission on the Way: Issues in Mission Theology*. Grand Rapids: Baker Books, 1996.

_____. *Growth of the True Church*. Amsterdam: Rodopi, 1981.

Van Engen, Charles, Dean S Gilliland, and Paul Pierson (eds). *The Good News of the Kingdom* Congratulatory ed. Maryknoll: Orbis Books, 1993.

Vanhoozer, Kevin J. *Dictionary for Theological Interpretation of the Bible*. Grand Rapids, MI: Baker Academic, 2005.

Wagner, Peter C. *Acts of the Holy Spirit: A Modern Commentary on the Book of Acts*. California: Regel, 1994.

_____. *Called and Empowered: Global Mission in Pentecostal Perspective,* (Peabody, MA: Hendrickson Publishers, 1991.

_____. *Your Church Can Be Healthy.* Nashville: Abingdon Press, 1979.

Walker, Michael. *The Work of the Spirit: Pneumatology and Pentecostalism.* Grand Rapids: Eerdmans Publication, 2006.

Walls, Andrew and Cathy Ross. *Mission in the 21st Century.* Maryknoll, NY: Orbis Books, 2008.

Walvoord, John F. *Jesus Christ Our Lord.* Chicago: Moody Press, 1969.

Wan, Enoch. "A Comparative Study of Sino-American Cognitive, Theological Pattern, and Proposed Alternative." www.enochwan.com/English/articles/relational_paradigm.html (Accessed September 15, 2016).

_____. "Core Values of Mission Organization in the Cultural Context of the 21st Century." www.globalmissiology.org Featured Article, Published January 2009.

_____. *Diaspora Missiology: Theory, Methodology, and Practice.* Portland: Institute of Diaspora Studies, 2011.

_____. "Holistic Ministry/Missions: Reflections and Resource Materials." http://www.enochwan.com/english/articles/pdf/Holistic%20Ministry%20Missions.pdf (Accessed May 15, 2015).

_____. "Inter-Disciplinary and Integrative Missiological Research, The What, Why, and How." www.globalmissiology.org Published July 2017.

_____. "Relational Theology and Relational Missiology," *Occasional Bulletin* vol 21, no 1. Wheaton: Evangelical Missiological Society, 2013.

_____. "Rethinking Missiological Research Methodology: Exploring a New Direction." Evangelical Theological Soc./Evangelical Missiological Soc. Regional Meeting. Columbia Intl. U, Columbia, SC. 20-21 Mar. 1998. Portland, OR: Theological Research Exchange Network, n.d. ETS-0494 (Accessed May 15, 2015).

_____. "Spiritual Warfare and Victorious Christian." http://www.enochwan.com/english/articles/pdf/Spiritual%20Warfare%20&%20Victorious%20Christian.pdf (Accessed November 27, 2017).

_____. "Spiritual Warfare: Understanding Demonization." http://ojs.globalmissiology.org/index.php/english/article/view/443/1144 (Accessed December 05, 2017).

_____. "The Paradigm of 'Relational Realism,'" *Occasional Bulletin.* Wheaton: Evangelical Missiological Society, Spring 2006b.

Warren, Rick. *The Purpose Driven Church: Growth Without Compromising Your Message and Mission.* Grand Rapids: Zondervan, 1995.

Washer, Paul. *The Gospel's Power and Message.* Grand Rapids: Reformation Heritage Books, 2012.

Webster, John. "Principles of Systematic Theology," *International Journal of Systematic Theology* 11, no.1 (January 2009), 61-62.

Williams, J Rodman. *The Gift of the Holy Spirit Today.* Plainfield, NJ: Logos International, 1980.

Willis, Wendell (ed). *The Kingdom of God in 20th Century Interpretation.* Peabody, MA: Hendrickson Publishers, 1987.

Wilson, S G. *The Gentiles and the Gentile Mission in Luke – Acts.* Cambridge: Cambridge University Press, 1973.

Winter, Ralph D and Steven Hawthorne (eds). *Perspectives on the World Christian Movement:A Reader,* 3rd ed. Pasadena: William Carey Library, 2009.

Woodall, Chris. *Atonement: God's Means of Effecting Man's Reconciliation.* Eugene, OR: Wipf and Stock, 2015.

Wright, Christopher J. "Re-affirming Holistic Mission: A Cross-Centered Approach in All Areas of Life." https://www.lausanneworldpulse.com/themedarticles-php/61/10-2005 (Accessed May 12, 2015).

_____. *The Mission of God, Unlocking the Bible's Grand Narrative.* Downers Grove, IL: InterVarsity Press, 2006.

Wycliffe. "The History of Wycliffe." https://www.wycliffe.org/about (Accessed December 16, 2017).

Yoder, John Howard. *Theology of Mission.* Downers Grove: IVP Academic, 2014.

Yohannan, K.P. *Why the World Waits: Exposing the Reality of Modern Missions.* Lake Mary, FL: Creation House, 1991.

_____. *Revolution in World Missions.* Carrollton, TX: GFA Books, 2001.

Yong, Amos. *Who is the Holy Spirit? A Walk with the Apostles.* Brewster, MA: Paraclete Press, 2011.

_____. "The Spirit of Science: Are Pentecostals Ready to Engage the Discussion?" http://www.pctii.org/cyberj/cyberj20/yong.html (Accessed July 10, 2017).

_____. *Spirit-Word Community: Theological Hermeneutics in Trinitarian Perspective.* Burlington, VT: Ashgate Publishing, 1988, 2002.

York, John V. *Missions in the Age of the Spirit.* Springfield: Gospel Publishing House, 2000.

Zacharias, Ravi. "Why this Muslim-turned-Christian speaker resonated with so many before his death at 34." https://www.washingtonpost.com/amphtml/news/acts-of-faith/wp/2017/09/17/why-this-muslim-turned-christian-speaker-resonated-with-so-many-before-his-death-at-34 (Accessed October 05, 2017).

Zuk, Roy B (ed). *Vital Missions Issues: Examining Challenges and Changes in World Evangelism.* Grand Rapids: Kregel Resources, 1998.

Zukeran, Patrick. "The Apologetics of Jesus." https://bible.org/article/apologetics-jesus Published September 25, 2009. (Accessed December 16, 2017).

Center for Diaspora and Relational Research ("CDDR")

Western Seminary Press

Diaspora Missiology Series

D1   Italian Diaspora意大利散聚華人及散聚宣教 (C)

D2   Towards a Field Support Ministry Guidebook: An Integrative Study on Chinese Diaspora Kingdom Workers in a Creative Access Region (E)

D3   Engaging Chinese Diaspora in the Ministry of Bible Translation (E)

D4   Diaspora Missions to International Students (E)

D5   Missions Beyond the Diaspora: Local Cross-cultural Ministry of Chinese Congregations in the San Francisco Bay Area (E)

D6   Multiethnic Ministries and Diaspora Missions in Action: A Case Study of the Wu Chang Church of Kaosiung, Taiwan (E)

Relational Research Series

R1   Engaging the Secular World through Life-on-life Disciple-making in the British Context: Relational Paradigm in Action (E)

R2   A Theology of Spirit-Anointed Witness in Holistic Christian Mission Framed in the Relational Paradigm (E)

NOTE: (C) – publication in Chinese
(E) – publication in English

The titles listed above are a both in-print and e-book, available @ Amazon.com